FIRST CORINTHIANS

ALFRED MARTIN

FIRST CORINTHIANS

ALFRED MARTIN

LOIZEAUX BROTHERS

Neptune, New Jersey

First Corinthians
© 1989 by Alfred Martin. All rights reserved.

Printed in the United States of America.
A publication of Loizeaux Brothers, Inc., a nonprofit
organization devoted to the Lord's work and to the
spread of his truth.

Library of Congress Cataloging-in-Publication Data

Martin, Alfred, 1916-
    First Corinthians/Alfred Martin.
        p.   cm.
    Includes bibliographical references.
    ISBN 0-87213-644-2
    1. Bible. N. T. Corinthians, 1st—Commentaries.
I. Title.
II. Title: 1st Corinthians.
BS2675.3.M37   1990   89-35934
227'.207—dc20   CIP

This commentary is based on the New King James
Version and all scripture quotations (unless otherwise
indicated) are from that version, copyright 1979, 1980,
1982, 1985 by Thomas Nelson, Inc., Nashville,
Tennessee. Used by permission.

CONTENTS

Preface		7
Introduction		9
PART ONE.	**Problems about Which Paul Had Heard**	
	1 Corinthians 1–6	17
Problem One.	Divisions	
	1 Corinthians 1–4	19
Problem Two.	Discipline	
	1 Corinthians 5–6	51
PART TWO.	**Things the Corinthians Had Written to Paul**	
	1 Corinthians 7–16	67
Subject One.	Marriage, Separation and Divorce	
	1 Corinthians 7	69
Subject Two.	Christian Liberty	
	1 Corinthians 8–10	83
Subject Three.	Order in the Church	
	1 Corinthians 11	100
Subject Four.	Spiritual Gifts	
	1 Corinthians 12–14	108
Subject Five.	Resurrection	
	1 Corinthians 15	128
Subject Six.	The Collection and Other Matters	
	1 Corinthians 16:1-11	143
Subject Seven.	Concerning Apollos and Closing Greetings	
	1 Corinthians 16:12-24	146

Appendix: Notes on Apostolic Chronology   151

Select Bibliography   153

Scripture Index   157

PREFACE

When Paul wrote his epistle to the Romans he was staying in the home of a man named Gaius in Corinth (Romans 16:23). The dreadful conditions described in the opening section of Romans certainly could find illustration in the daily life of Corinth. First Corinthians, probably written a year before Romans, also paints an unflattering portrait of Greco-Roman civilization.

Yet both of these great letters are filled with the joyous confidence that the gospel of the Lord Jesus Christ is more than adequate to conquer sin and Satan. "And such were some of you," Paul wrote with undoubted emphasis on the past tense. "But you were washed, but you were sanctified, but you were justified in the name of the Lord Jesus and by the Spirit of our God" (1 Corinthians 6:11).

This book is not a technical exegetical verse-by-verse commentary on 1 Corinthians, but it does seek to convey the meaning of this inspired letter and to help the serious student of the scriptures interpret and apply its contents.

The more I have studied 1 Corinthians through the years and the more times I have taught it to Bible college students, the more I have recognized the similarities between the culture of first-century Corinth and the culture of today. With thanks to God that the gospel is still "the power of God to salvation for every one who believes" (Romans 1:16), let us resolve to place before everyone and everything else "Jesus Christ and Him crucified" (1 Corinthians 2:2).

INTRODUCTION

If the presence of the apostle Paul brought so much good to individuals and churches, how much more did his absence contribute to their growth and development in Christ. The apostle's oral ministry was helpful and effective, but limited by time and space. His written ministry remains forever as a part of God's inspired, inerrant word. Believers through the centuries have found, and will continue to find, the guidance and strength needed for Christian living and service. We can be thankful that we are not dependent on the mere remembrance of something we have heard in the past, but that we have the objective word of God, "which lives and abides forever" (1 Peter 1:23). In the marvelous providence of God, we have multiplied copies available to us in our own language and in reliable versions.

A frequently expressed wish among believers of our day is that we might have a "New Testament church," free from the accretions of centuries and the unbiblical changes that have entered in the course of history. We might well ask, however, "Which New Testament church?" Do we want to have the doctrinal aberrations of the churches of Galatia or even of Colosse? Certainly no one would deliberately ask to have a church like that in Corinth. It would be difficult to imagine a church with more problems than that one. The wrangling over human teachers, the intense party spirit, the continuing condition of spiritual babyhood, the amazing toleration of flagrant immorality in the church fellowship, the use of the pagan law courts for settling quarrels among believers, the participation in heathen rites and ceremonies, the acceptance of sexual sin as of little consequence, the serious abuse of spiritual gifts, the denial of bodily resurrection, including the essential doctrine of the resurrection of the Lord Jesus Christ himself—all these problems and more were evident among this unruly assembly of converts from raw paganism.

No local church is perfect, but by God's grace we can improve the churches of our day if we will heed the teaching we encounter in scripture. Even the mistakes and errors of the Corinthian church can be warning examples to us of what not to do.

Paul first visited Corinth on his second missionary journey, after his experiences in Athens. The historical background of his sojourn is found in Acts 18:1-18, where we read also that in Corinth the Lord Jesus personally appeared to him and encouraged him by revealing that he had many people in that city (18:9-10).

What a city! In Paul's day Corinth was both a very old city and a relatively new city.

It was old, because for centuries it had straddled the Isthmus of Corinth, that narrow neck of land joining the northern part of what we call Greece, and the southern peninsula, traditionally called the Peloponnesus (the "island of Pelops," although of course it was not an island). At that location Corinth commanded the land routes from north to south, and also the sea routes to the east through the Saronic Gulf and the Aegean Sea, and to the west (and to Rome) through the Gulf of Corinth and the Adriatic.

Corinth was mentioned at least as early as the Homeric poems, with an importance based in large measure on its strategic location. Homer referred to it as "wealthy Corinth" (*Iliad*, ii, 570).

It was later a leading member of the Greek city-states, which banded together under the leadership—actually the military coercion—of King Philip of Macedon, ostensibly to oppose the titanic Persian Empire, but also to assure the military dominance of Macedon over the varied and often warring Greek city-states. This Achaean (Hellenic or Greek) League survived Philip's assassination. His son, Alexander the Great, was invested at Corinth with the presidency of the League and led its forces in a spectacular invasion and defeat of the sprawling Persian Empire (334–322 B.C.).

The old city of Corinth, therefore, had a history going back to distant antiquity. Its strategic location and impressive terrain contributed to its importance. The rocky mountain standing guard over the city, the Acrocorinthus, gave the location a striking uniqueness. Rising to 1,887 feet (575 meters), this unusual hill served as the acropolis or citadel. No doubt from early times there had been a temple of Aphrodite, the Greek goddess of love and beauty (roughly corresponding to the Roman Venus), on this spot. The first-century Greek geographer, Strabo (64 or 63 B.C.–after A.D. 23), so indicates.

But Corinth, the old city, had been completely destroyed by the Roman general Lucius Mummius in 146 B.C. The power-hungry senate of the Roman Republic, considering it a danger to Rome's hegemony in the eastern Mediterranean world, brought the Achaean League to an end. For a century this once great and famous city lay desolate, leveled to the ground.

Julius Caesar, the Roman dictator, was responsible for its rebuilding in the middle of the first century B.C. His orders were given shortly before his assassination, which occurred on March 15, 44 B.C. Caesar wanted the city to serve as a reminder to the Greeks of the power of their Roman conquerors. He also designated the city a Roman colony, thus making possible the settlement there of numerous Roman army veterans. Philippi in Macedonia also was such a colony (Acts 16:12).

Consequently, when Paul came to Corinth about a century after its rebuilding, scarcely any buildings in the city were more than a hundred years old. It is useless to speculate whether the new Corinth should be considered a Greek city or a Roman city. It was undoubtedly both—Greek in geographical location, in ancient cultural heritage, and in philosophical tradition, but decidedly Roman in its form of government, its bustling trade and commerce, and the "progressiveness" of its cosmopolitan culture. Edwards speaks of Corinth as "the least Greek of Greek cities and the least Roman of Roman colonies." Actually it had some of the good features and all of the worst features of both Greek and Roman cities, plus characteristics of cities from the east. It was indeed a melting pot. Barrett's statement, "It is impossible to think of the Corinth of Paul's day as in any way distinctively Greek," seems too strong in view of the philosophical and practical overtones now to be mentioned.

Besides, any such characterization can be only partially true. Many features of Corinth were typical of Greece, such as the general interest in oratory and rhetoric, the avid following of athletic contests, the search after wisdom (after all, philosophy as we know it originated with the Greeks), and the interest in cultic religion as exemplified by the temple and worship of Aphrodite.

It was a truism in the ancient Roman world that while Rome conquered Greece externally, Greece conquered Rome inwardly. The Romans were amalgamators and improvisers, incorporating the most powerful and useful features of the various cultural backgrounds and ethnic groups of the people they included in their sphere of influence.

The Greek peninsula was divided by the Roman overlords into two senatorial provinces: Macedonia in the north, taking in the former kingdom of Macedon and the surrounding area and including the great cities of Philippi, Thessalonica, Berea, and others, and Achaia in the south with its capital at Corinth. By Paul's day these two provinces had become imperial entities, directly accountable to the emperor through his vicegerent, called in Roman law a *proconsul*, one who served in place of a consul (retaining the old forms of republican Rome, but investing them with entirely different meaning).The proconsul Gallio is mentioned in Acts 18:12. He was a half-brother of the well-known Stoic philosopher Seneca, Nero's tutor.

At any rate, the Corinth of Paul's day was a large city by first-century standards. No census figures are available, but estimates of both ancient and modern authorities place the population of first-century Corinth anywhere between one hundred thousand and six hundred thousand, with the larger figure possibly nearer the truth. It was obviously a commercial center, a gateway both to the Asiatic east and to the European west and of course to the great capital,which boasted that "all roads lead to Rome." Although not in the first rank of cities like Rome, Alexandria, and Syrian Antioch, Corinth was nevertheless one of the great centers of civilization.

The city was overrun with sailors, traveling salesmen, merchants, traders, itinerant philosophers, and purveyors of ancient and modern cults, especially of the "mystery religions," which had such a vogue in the eastern Mediterranean region.

In our day a canal connects the Aegean and the Adriatic ports of Corinth. Attempts to construct such a canal in ancient times were not successful. In the first century it was closer, quicker, and even cheaper to unload a ship's cargo at the eastern side, transport it overland to the western side and reload it on a ship there (or the reverse process) than it was to take the long and dangerous voyage around Cape Malea at the southern tip of the Peloponnesus. Some smaller ships were actually placed on rollers

and were pushed and pulled all the way across the is
Cenchrea, on the east side of the isthmus, was about seve
from the city center (Acts 18:18; Romans 16:1), and Leche
the northwest, was less than two miles from Corinth.

It seems that a transient population is more conducive to
moral laxity than a more settled culture is. Even the ancient
pagan Greeks had in their vocabulary the word *Corinthiazesthai*,
"to live like a Corinthian," that is, "to live a licentious and
immoral life." This term is at least as old as the time of the comic
dramatist, Aristophanes (ca. 450–388 B.C.).

The mid-first-century Roman Empire can be compared with
many features of late twentieth-century western European and
American culture. Not the least of these traits are the breakdown
of public and private morals, the openness and blatancy of personal sexual immorality, the destruction of the family (God's ear-
liest institution), the practice of abortion and infanticide, the
prevalence and ease of divorce, and the widespread acceptance
of homosexuality as an "alternative lifestyle."

Greek life and religion were permeated with sex. Ancient
Corinth was said to have had a temple of Aphrodite in which there
were a "thousand priestesses," (read it "prostitutes"). Whether
the temple of Aphrodite in Paul's day was this extensive is uncertain, but the same religious practices were undoubtedly
widespread. It was a recognized part of the "fertility cults" to try
to make sexual intercourse with these priestesses an act of worship. Wives in Greek culture often were legally honored but
ignored in practice in the conduct of affairs of state and in much
of the social life of the day. It was a "man's world" in the worst
sense of the term, built to a large extent on both heterosexual and
homosexual immorality.

The latter feature, which had been an integral part of pagan
Greek life for centuries, was the so-called "Greek love"
(*paederasty*), a flagrant form of homosexual activity reminiscent
of the condemned city of Sodom (Genesis 19) and the depraved
behavior of the men of Gibeah (Judges 19), resurfacing in the culture of our day. As an illustration of how these practices permeated the ancient Greek culture, one can see with amazement and
repugnance how even great thinkers such as Socrates and Plato
took such behavior for granted as an accepted part of life, as Plato
described in his dialogue, *The Symposium*. The participants in
that dialogue, including Socrates, agreed that homosexual love

between men and boys is a higher and more spiritual form of love than that between men and women.

THE PLACE OF 1 CORINTHIANS AMONG PAUL'S WRITINGS

The chronology of Paul's life and of the New Testament in general is not yet an exact science. There are wide differences of opinion about many of the dates, and few fixed points by which to calculate the time of particular events. The following plan is based in large part on J.B. Lightfoot's reconstruction, which many consider outmoded or superseded by the views of Sir William Ramsay. The dating proposed by Boyer in the *Wycliffe Bible Encyclopedia* places the death of Paul in 64 or 65 A.D., which does not seem to allow enough time for a release from a first Roman imprisonment, an interval of ministry, and a final imprisonment leading to martyrdom. For further discussion of the chronology see the Appendix.

The thirteen epistles of the apostle Paul fall into four chronological groups.

GROUP ONE: Epistles of the Second Missionary Journey

    1 Thessalonians (probably A.D. 52)
    2 Thessalonians (probably A.D. 52)
    General Theme: The Return of the Lord
    Type: Eschatological Epistles

GROUP TWO: Epistles of the Third Missionary Journey

    Galatians (probably A.D. 55)
    1 Corinthians (probably A.D. 57, Spring)
    2 Corinthians (probably A.D. 57, Fall)
    Romans (probably A.D. 58)
    General Theme: The Gospel and Its Implications
    Type: Soteriological Epistles

GROUP THREE: Epistles of the First Roman Imprisonment

    Ephesians (probably A.D. 62)
    Colossians (probably A.D. 62)
    Philemon (probably A.D. 62)

Philippians (probably A.D. 63)
General Theme: Christ the Head of the Body, the Church
Type: Christological Epistles

GROUP FOUR: Epistles of the Interim and of the Second Roman
              Imprisonment

1 Timothy (probably A.D. 65)
Titus (probably A.D. 65)
2 Timothy (probably A.D. 68)
General Theme: Instructions for Pastors (The Pastoral Epistles)
Type: Ecclesiological Epistles

It is the second group that especially claims our attention in this study.

Romans is the great systematic treatise on the gospel. Galatians deals with the same subject polemically or argumentatively, combating and refuting the errors of false teachers, particularly of the Judaizers. First and 2 Corinthians show how the gospel affects the daily life and conduct of the believer. First Corinthians is often called "practical." This does not mean that the epistle is contrary to doctrine or that doctrine is impractical.

Although each epistle has its own distinctive theme, there is a uniformity among those of each group.

THE THEME OF 1 CORINTHIANS

First Corinthians is definitely an epistle of correction. Paul found many things about Corinth that needed to be changed. One of the lessons to be discovered in this epistle is that the gospel of the Lord Jesus Christ affects every area of life. Consequently, one might express the theme as: *the gospel in its personal, practical, and social implications.*

While the gospel is stated clearly in 1 Corinthians (e.g., 2:2, and, above all, 15:1-5), the epistle stresses that conduct which ought to flow from the gospel. Even though 1 Corinthians was probably written before Romans, it follows Romans logically as being based on the teaching of that great doctrinal epistle.

We are taught in 2 Timothy 3:16 that "all Scripture is given by inspiration of God, and is profitable . . ." While the areas of use-fulness are all applicable in some measure to every part of the Bible, various parts have special emphases. The word *correction* seems particularly applicable to 1 Corinthians. Obviously the other elements are treated also.

THE STRUCTURE OF THE EPISTLE

Although the contents of the epistle do not seem to fall into as logical a pattern as Romans, careful study will reveal groupings of topics and a continuous and connected flow of thought. The overall outline is quite simple. In the first part (chapters 1–6) of the epistle Paul wrote about matters he had heard concerning the Corinthians (1 Corinthians 1:11); in the second part (chapters 7–16) he specifically answered questions concerning which the Corinthian church had written to him (1 Corinthians 7:1).

Problem solving is very popular in the culture of the late twen-tieth century. Because this is a problem-solving epistle, it should be especially applicable to our day. In fact, the more one reads this epistle, the more one sees similarities between the culture of Paul's day and the culture of our time.

The problem solving in this epistle, however, is not of human devising but of divine instruction. Paul had authority from God to tell the Corinthians, sometimes bluntly and even painfully but always lovingly and plainly, where they were wrong and how they could get right—right with God and right with one another.

PART ONE

Problems
about which
Paul Had Heard
1 Corinthians 1–6

PROBLEM ONE
Divisions
1 Corinthians 1–4

THE APOSTLE'S GREETING (1:1–3)

1:1 Paul, called to be an apostle of Jesus Christ through the will of God, and Sosthenes our brother,

1:2 To the church of God which is at Corinth, to those who are sanctified in Christ Jesus, called to be saints, with all who in every place call on the name of Jesus Christ our Lord, both theirs and ours:

1:3 Grace to you and peace from God our Father and the Lord Jesus Christ.

Many leaders and founders of religions have written learned and often obscure tracts, treatises, and dissertations. The apostles of Christ "wrote letters to the brethren." God's instruction of his children is intensely practical. Yet one cannot say that this epistle or any other New Testament writing is simplistic. We marvel that the first-century Christians, many of whom were illiterate and uneducated, could apparently understand great doctrinal truths. This testifies to the illuminating ministry of the Holy Spirit to those believers who truly want to know and understand God's word.

Paul followed the general form for introducing a letter in his day. First he identified himself, authenticating his message. He was no stranger to many of the Corinthian believers, for he had lived among them for almost two years. Although probably several years had passed since he had last seen them, the ties were deep and tender. He was their spiritual father (1 Corinthians 4:15) and he had not forgotten them for a moment.

Paul identified himself as one who had been specially called and sent by God. The term *apostle* is almost always used in the New Testament in its technical sense, not as a general term like our expression "missionary," although the meanings are the same. Acts 14: 14 seems to be an exception. When Paul called himself an apostle it was because God had called him to that holy office, "through the will of God." The word *called* is not our English idea of "named," but indicates the divine appointment, akin to "chose" and "appointed" in John 15:16.

"Sosthenes our brother"—was this the same Sosthenes as in Acts 18:17, the "ruler of the synagogue"? Possibly so. It is enjoyable to speculate about how difficult it may have been for the unbelieving Jews of Corinth to keep men in the office of "chief ruler of the synagogue." First Crispus became a Christian (Acts 18:8), and then possibly Sosthenes. Abundant grace! The inclusion of Sosthenes' name does not mean that he was a coauthor of the epistle. Paul customarily joined his name with those of dear friends known to his readers who were with him at the time he wrote. He later revealed that he was writing this letter during his extended stay in Ephesus on his third missionary journey (1 Corinthians 16:8). How or why Sosthenes had joined him there we are not told, but obviously this particular Sosthenes was well known to Paul's readers. That he was a Christian is clear from the expression "our brother," which Paul normally used for believers, although Acts 22:1 is an exception.

In a Pauline salutation the persons addressed were named and usually identified in some distinctive manner: "To the church of God which is at Corinth." Scripture uses this word (literally "assembly"or "the called-out entity") for the whole body of Christ, all believers everywhere, the "church universal" (hence the expression used by the church fathers, "the holy catholic church"); scripture also uses this word for the local church, the assembly of believers in a particular area. Although some have denied one usage and some the other, the New Testament seems clearly to recognize and use the expression in both of these ways. Some passages in which the Greek word is used for local assemblies are Galatians 1:2; 1 Thessalonians 1:1; 2 Thessalonians 1:1; Acts 20:17; and Revelation 1:4. Reference to the universal church is made in such passages as Matthew 16:18; 1 Corinthians 10:32; Ephesians 3:10; and others. The reader is referred to a complete concordance for further study.

Paul frequently included along with the geographical location ("at Corinth") the spiritual position of those to whom he wrote ("in Christ Jesus").

In the light of what is said later about the faults and sins of the Corinthian believers, it is essential that their established position in Christ be thoroughly understood. This is reinforced by the participle *sanctified* and the noun *saints,* both from the same root, meaning literally "those set apart" or "those declared holy" and "set-apart ones" or "holy ones." Scripture views the doctrine of sanctification in three ways. Every believer has been sanctified, or set apart, positionally from the moment he believes (Hebrews 10:10-14). The Holy Spirit is conducting a progressive work of sanctification, or experiential sanctification, in the believer throughout this life (1 Thessalonians 4:3; 2 Timothy 2:21; Hebrews 10:14). Complete and ultimate sanctification will come at the appearing of the Lord Jesus to gather his own to himself (1 John 3:1-3).

In contrast to the widespread view that Christians are in the process of becoming saints or that they may someday be declared saints by church or priestly authority, the New Testament identifies all believers as saints. The admonition is not, "Live a holy life so that you can become a saint," but, "God has already made you a saint; now live as a saint should live." Many of the Corinthians were anything but saintly in their conduct, as is also true of many of us. But through the sanctifying work of the Holy Spirit we are gradually being conformed to the image of Christ; in other words, our state is being brought into harmony with our standing in Christ.

The closing words of the address remind us that although this is a special epistle addressed to believers who are in the church at Corinth, in definite situations and with definite problems, it has application to any and all believers at any and all times: "all who in every place call on the name of Jesus Christ our Lord, both theirs and ours." We have a union and a fellowship with one another because of our common allegiance to the Lord Jesus Christ.

Paul's salutations were never complete without his benediction. He seems to have been directed by the Holy Spirit to transform the usual greeting into a definite gospel message. The normal greeting in a letter such as this uses the infinitive *chairein* from the root meaning "rejoice." Note this greeting in James 1:1

and in the two letters in Acts 15:23 and 23:26.

Paul used the beautiful related word *charis,* "grace," and poured into it a depth of meaning it did not have in the older Greek. It is similar in meaning to the Hebrew word *chen,* as in Genesis 6:8. In biblical usage it carries the thought of God's unmerited favor shown toward those who deserve only his judgment. It is "undeserved, unearned, and unrecompensed" (L.S. Chafer).

Along with this preeminently New Testament greeting the apostle joined the traditional Old Testament greeting of "peace" (Hebrew *shalom,* Greek *eirene*). All thirteen of Paul's epistles contain this formula, but the three pastoral epistles add the word *mercy* in the Traditional Text: 1 Timothy 1:2; 2 Timothy 1:2; and Titus 1:4. (See NKJV; cf. *The Greek New Testament According to the Majority Text.*)

The grammatical connection between "God our Father" and "the Lord Jesus Christ" shows the unity and the identity of the persons who are the source of grace and peace.

PAUL'S THANKSGIVING FOR THE CORINTHIANS (1:4-9)

1:4 I thank my God always concerning you for the grace of God which was given to you by Christ Jesus,
1:5 that you were enriched in everything by Him in all utterance and all knowledge,
1:6 even as the testimony of Christ was confirmed in you,
1:7 so that you come short in no gift, eagerly waiting for the revelation of our Lord Jesus Christ,
1:8 who will also confirm you to the end, that you may be blameless in the day of our Lord Jesus Christ.
1:9 God is faithful, by whom you were called into the fellowship of His Son, Jesus Christ our Lord.

Paul customarily thanked God at the outset of his letters for the people to whom he was writing. Galatians is an exception, for in those churches the depth of the doctrinal error was so alarming that the apostle, evidently feeling there was little at that point to give thanks about, plunged immediately into his theme of warning the churches against a serious and tragic heresy.

Indeed, Corinth had its serious problems, but they were errors in practice more than in doctrine, and at least the apostle could thank God for what he had already done for them. This was, after all, a church that had been greatly endowed and greatly blessed by God. The word *enriched* reminded them of all that God had done. They had a ministry ("utterance") both to saved and unsaved rising out of what they had received personally from the Holy Spirit of God: "knowledge." This word has particular significance in the light of what is seen later about the faint beginnings of that heresy known as gnosticism which came into greater prominence in the church at the beginning of the second century. In contrast to the false claim to knowledge, introduced and propagated with misguided zeal by these early heretics (1 Timothy 6:20), is the true knowledge imparted to believers by the Holy Spirit of God.

Furthermore, the Corinthians were recipients of God's sovereign dispensing of gifts (an area covered at some length in 1 Corinthians 12–14). Note that they had been especially blessed by God in this area, "so that you come short in no gift."

They were also an expectant church, "eagerly waiting for the revelation of our Lord Jesus Christ" (1:7). Paul's confidence did not rest on what the Corinthians had done or would do, but on the faithfulness of God (1:9).

Paul's Plea for Unity (1:10-17)

1:10 Now I plead with you, brethren, by the name of our Lord Jesus Christ, that you all speak the same thing, and that there be no divisions among you, but that you be perfectly joined together in the same mind and in the same judgment.

1:11 For it has been declared to me concerning you, my brethren, by those of Chloe's household, that there are contentions among you.

1:12 Now I say this, that each of you says, "I am of Paul," or "I am of Apollos," or "I am of Cephas," or "I am of Christ."

1:13 Is Christ divided? Was Paul crucified for you? Or were you baptized in the name of Paul?

1:14 I thank God that I baptized none of you except Crispus and Gaius,

1:15 lest anyone should say that I had baptized in my own name.

1:16 Yes, I also baptized the household of Stephanas. Besides, I do not know whether I baptized any other.

1:17 For Christ did not send me to baptize, but to preach the gospel, not with wisdom of words, lest the cross of Christ should be made of no effect.

What Paul had heard concerning the Corinthians soon came to the fore as he urged them earnestly to "speak the same thing." The divisions were evident and deep. The word *schismata* is properly translated "divisions." These divisions were leading to outbreaks of strife (*erides*). The spiritual atmosphere had become tense.

We do not know who Chloe was, nor who were the members of her household. Possibly these friends had come from Corinth to Ephesus on business, not necessarily especially to bring a message to Paul; but having found him, they no doubt had much to tell, and he had many questions about his beloved converts.

The contentions centered around preferences for human teachers. It is often hard to explain or even to understand why one prefers the manner and content of one man's teaching above another. Part of it, no doubt, lies in the elusive personality of the individual hearer, who "knows what he likes," often without being able to articulate why he has this preference.

Some have conjectured that what some people liked especially about Paul was his logical and profound argumentation. He soon tells us, however, that his presence among the Corinthians had not depended on deeply theological or philosophical preaching, but on a straightforward presentation of the unadulterated gospel (2:2).

Apollos evidently was a Hellenistic Jew. Scripture says he came from Alexandria. He is described as "an eloquent man and mighty in the Scriptures" (Acts 18:24). No doubt his eloquence was deeply appreciated by many in the Corinthian church.

Peter, or Cephas, would be representative of the true Hebrew Christians, although all three of the men mentioned were Christians of Hebrew descent. But his personality no doubt appealed to some more than others. The fact that Peter was one of the twelve apostles would certainly impress some.

Paul likely used these names not as an exhaustive list, but as a representative one. Whatever else they were doing, the Corinthians were following human leaders on the basis of mere human preference.

But what about the fourth group? These may have been the self-righteous, self-satisfied ones. "No," they may have been saying, "we would not follow any man as the head of a faction in the church; we will follow Christ."

In so saying and so doing, they were not exalting the Lord Jesus, but were bringing him down to the level of the others: the leader of a party or faction. "I am of Christ." This was probably said smugly and judgmentally, with the thought, "I am better than you are, because I follow Christ, not Paul or Apollos or Peter (Cephas) or any merely human leader."

The questions that Paul asked at this point were very searching and very conclusive. The Greek negative *me* was used, an idiomatic expression which in asking a question requires the answer no. "Christ is not divided, is he?" "Paul was not crucified for you, was he?" "You were not baptized in the name of Paul, were you?"

Baptism, as will be seen later in this epistle, has identification as its central idea. The Lord Jesus, in giving what has come to be called the baptismal formula, spoke of being baptized in (or into) the name of the Father, the Son, and the Holy Spirit (Matthew 28:19), and this identification is said to be a mystical union with the Lord Jesus Christ. "For as many of you as were baptized into Christ have put on Christ" (Galatians 3:27). Consequently Paul was making it clear that he was not bringing converts into identification with himself, but with the Lord Jesus Christ alone. This is why he was thankful that he did not baptize many people—not that he considered baptism as of no importance, but that it was secondary to the proclamation of the saving gospel of Christ.

Some ultradispensationalists have tried to use 1:17 to bolster their contention that baptism is not for the church age. What Paul was saying, of course, was that baptizing was not his primary mission. What he was to do above anything and everything else was to preach the gospel. But even in this passage he enumerated some whom he did baptize.

Many have professed difficulty in seeing the connection of

thoughts here. Paul seems to jump from the man-named divisions into a different topic: a contrast between two kinds of wisdom.

The connection, though not obvious at first, is really not difficult to discover. The divisions, named for various human leaders, arose out of a display of the wrong kind of wisdom, which Paul calls "the wisdom of this world." This is in direct contrast to the true wisdom, "the wisdom of God," which is described and honored in many places in scripture.

"Wisdom of words" (1:17) was well known and devoutly practiced among the Greek philosophers, especially by those who came to be known as "sophists," who were always ready on any occasion to argue long and vehemently on any side of any question, usually for a price. This has been memorialized in English in the word *sophistry* and its cognates, sophistry being defined as "subtly deceptive reasoning or argumentation" (*Webster's Ninth New Collegiate Dictionary*).

The lesson in this is that the simple, straightforward message of the cross must not be altered or adulterated in any way. In that message is found the true wisdom, as distinguished from the false wisdom of the world (*kosmos* or "world system"). This is in wonderful harmony with the Old Testament wisdom literature, particularly with the book of Proverbs. Wisdom is seen in the Bible as the proper use of knowledge in subjection to the will of God. It has a moral quality as well as an intellectual quality.

CHRIST, THE WISDOM OF GOD (1:18-25)

1:18 For the message of the cross is foolishness to those who are perishing, but to us who are being saved it is the power of God.

1:19 For it is written:
"I will destroy the wisdom of the wise,
And bring to nothing the understanding of the prudent."

1:20 Where is the wise? Where is the scribe? Where is the disputer of this age? Has not God made foolish the wisdom of this world?

1:21 For since, in the wisdom of God, the world through wisdom did not know God, it pleased God through the foolishness of the message preached to save those who believe.

1:22 For Jews request a sign, and Greeks seek after wisdom;

1:23 but we preach Christ crucified, to the Jews a stumbling block and to the Greeks foolishness,

1:24 but to those who are called, both Jews and Greeks, Christ the power of God and the wisdom of God.

1:25 Because the foolishness of God is wiser than men, and the weakness of God is stronger than men.

Many people are deceived into thinking that what is obscure must also be profound. This accounts partially for the rapid growth of false cults and religions, whose mumbo jumbo or rigamarole of high-sounding words makes an impression on those who are looking for something strange and esoteric. In contrast, the gospel seems too simple to many people. Can a person actually be saved eternally just by believing that someone died on a cross many years ago? This is "foolishness to those who are perishing" (1:18), because it is contrary to the bent of the natural mind, which is in rebellion against God and supposes that everyone must always earn his own way.

The believer has been given an entirely different mind-set. This does not mean that he thinks illogically or irrationally. On the contrary, he now sees and thinks clearly. But he has crossed over from the world's side to God's side. Now, what he formerly thought was wisdom is clearly seen as the most arrant and egregious nonsense, and what he formerly thought was foolishness is now perceived as the most sublime and heavenly wisdom. These two "wisdoms" are antithetic. This is more than a mere paradox; it is a display of absolute contraries.

The "disputer of this age" who uses the "wisdom of this world" (1:20) is declared by God to be completely foolish. There are many areas of human learning in which an unsaved person can search out facts, often as well as a believer, but when one tries to reason about the facts pertaining to the origin, nature, and destiny of the universe apart from divine revelation one completely abandons the true wisdom.

Philosophy as we know it originated among the Greeks, who furnished some of the greatest thinkers of all time. *Philosophy* is literally the "love of wisdom." But the story of the development of philosophy is frustrating and ultimately leads to despair, because the answers to the most perplexing questions are never found through either human reason or human experience. The highest thought to which man can attain apart from the grace of God falls so far short of God's thinking that it can only be branded as "foolishness."

God, however, uses what the world calls "foolishness" in order to overcome the "wisdom of this world." How foolish it would seem to a proud philosopher to think that his intellectual attainments can get him nowhere, but that his only hope for time and eternity is found in a man who died on a cross!

The rendering of the KJV in 1:21 is somewhat misleading. It is not "the foolishness of preaching" (*keryxis*), as though the act of preaching were foolish, but "the foolishness of the message preached" (*kerygma*)—not the act of preaching as such, but the content of this particular proclamation.

The gospels show how the Jews were constantly asking the Lord Jesus for a sign, even when they saw the mighty miracles he was performing (Matthew 16:1). They were not content to hear his words. The Greeks, or gentiles, were constantly pursuing what they believed to be wisdom. A long line of philosophers taught among the Greeks from the classical period of Athens in the fifth century B.C. Socrates, who left no writings of his own, was interpreted through his most famous pupil, Plato, who in turn was followed by his most famous, but divergent pupil, Aristotle. Most philosophical questions that are known to our own day were aired, hotly debated, supported, and refuted by succeeding generations of philosophical scholars. They were always seeking wisdom, but never attaining it.

How it must have run counter to the pride of those intellectual giants, many of whom were also intellectual snobs, to be told that all of their vaunted wisdom was really foolishness and that the only true wisdom was to believe on someone who had died the vilest kind of criminal's death outside the relatively unknown city of Jerusalem. The cross always is and always will be an offense, a stumbling block, to the unsaved man. Various liberal theologians in the centuries since have tried to water down the message to make it more palatable to the hearers, but this has not worked and never will. There are innumerable kinds of false teaching abroad in the world, but all of these teachings fail in some respect to declare the truth concerning the person and work of the Lord Jesus Christ.

"But to those who are called . . ." No matter how well educated a person may be, if he has not received Christ as his savior, he has an intellectual blind spot. To such people the message of the cross cannot be anything else but foolishness. The Lord Jesus had anticipated this by his word to Nicodemus, "Unless one is born again, he cannot see the kingdom of God" (John 3:3). Those who are "called" are regenerated by the Spirit of God; they have a new birth from above; they become "a new creation" in Christ Jesus (2 Corinthians 5:17).

Christ becomes not only "wisdom" to those who accept him, but also "power." The Christian faith is not a static quality but a dynamic outlook which recognizes new life, an about-face that makes an individual a different person in quality while he remains the same person in identity. God is not limited to any one race or ethnic group. His power and his wisdom are manifested to non-Jews (Greeks, or gentiles) as well as to the covenant people of Israel.

Verse 25 expresses a paradox. The argument used appeals to human experience. God is not really foolish; because he is the perfect and infinite God, he could not possibly be. But if God could be foolish, even his "foolishness" would be infinitely wiser than the greatest human wisdom. Similarly, God is not really weak, nor could he possibly be. But if he could be weak, even his "weakness" would be infinitely more powerful than the greatest power of men.

ALL GLORY ONLY TO GOD (1:26-31)

1:26 For you see your calling, brethren, that not many wise according to the flesh, not many mighty, not many noble, are called.

1:27 But God has chosen the foolish things of the world to put to shame the wise, and God has chosen the weak things of the world to put to shame the things which are mighty;

1:28 and the base things of the world and the things which are despised God has chosen, and the things which are not, to bring to nothing the things that are,

1:29 that no flesh should glory in His presence.

> 1:30 But of Him you are in Christ Jesus, who became for
> us wisdom from God—and righteousness and sanc-
> tification and redemption—
> 1:31 that, as it is written, "He who glories, let him glory
> in the LORD."

Paul appealed to the experience of the Corinthians to show that
the gospel has not been most widely accepted among those
whom the world lauds and honors. Not many Platos or Aristotles
have accepted Christ, not many Caesars or Neros, not even many
Sauls of Tarsus. We must note that God does not say, "Not any";
he says, "Not many." The Countess of Huntington in the time of
the Wesleys liked to say that she was saved by an "m."

The multitude of first-century Christians were mostly little people by the world's reckoning, many of them the castoffs of
mankind by the usual worldly standards. But they were God's
real noblemen, God's truly wise, a divine aristocracy unknown to
those who strutted and fretted across the world's stage in places
of human leadership. Why? Because they believed God.

Because the gospel comes out of God's pure grace, no one can
boast of his salvation (Ephesians 2:8-10). "What do you have that
you did not receive?" (1 Corinthians 4:7). There will be absolutely no braggarts in heaven. Everyone who will be there will
be there because of Christ's blood, as a free gift (Romans 6:23).
All honor must go—and shall go—to God. None will go to men,
"that no flesh should glory in His presence." The apostle quoted
Jeremiah 9:24.

In Proverbs wisdom is personified, spoken of as though it were
a person. In that context wisdom is represented by a noble and
beautiful woman, because in Hebrew most abstract nouns are
feminine gender and the word for wisdom (*chokmah*) is feminine.
In the New Testament wisdom is not merely personified in a figurative sense, but is actually embodied in a person: the Lord
Jesus Christ himself. And that divine wisdom brings with it the
other qualities that are mentioned: righteousness, sanctification,
and redemption.

CHRIST'S PERSON AND WORK, THE HEART OF THE MESSAGE (2:1-5)

> 2:1 And I, brethren, when I came to you, did not come
> with excellence of speech or of wisdom declaring to
> you the testimony of God.

2:2 For I determined not to know anything among you except Jesus Christ and Him crucified.

2:3 I was with you in weakness, in fear, and in much trembling.

2:4 And my speech and my preaching were not with persuasive words of human wisdom, but in demonstration of the Spirit and of power,

2:5 that your faith should not be in the wisdom of men but in the power of God.

Paul next proceeded to explain how he had used and displayed the divine wisdom in his first appearing at Corinth. Some interpreters have believed that he made a serious mistake in Athens, that he had tried a philosophical approach which had not worked, and therefore he changed his entire plan of procedure at Corinth.

This is reading something into the text which is not there. The apostle's normal procedure, as he explains later in this epistle, was to "become all things to all men," that he "might by all means save some" (1 Corinthians 9:22). The fact that there were only a few saved in Athens does not prove that Paul used a totally wrong approach. He met the philosophers on their own ground and showed them the inadequacy of their philosophy. Scripture emphasizes that in Athens he preached "Jesus and the resurrection" (Acts 17:18). The crucifixion and the resurrection obviously go together. There is no doubt that in Athens Paul preached the substitutionary death of Christ as he also did in Corinth. It is inappropriate to criticize the words and actions of an apostle unless there is clear indication in scripture that he was out of harmony with the will of God.

The sophists prided themselves on their oratory, the type that could make even the most trivial subject sound as though it were the most important consideration in the universe. Paul came among the Corinthians declaring the clear gospel message in simple, but completely accurate and therefore powerful, language. The Traditional Text reads here, "the testimony of God," while the critical text as represented by the Aland-United Bible Societies reading has, "the mystery of God." Interestingly, NASB, NIV, and NKJV translators have all followed the traditional reading, even though in the case of the first two it is contrary to their usual textual preference.

Verse 2 gives us the heart of the gospel, for it concerns both the person and the redemptive work of Christ, "Jesus Christ and Him crucified,"—who Jesus Christ is, and what Jesus Christ has done. Did Paul mean that he literally did not know anything else? There are indications in scripture that he was a highly educated, extremely intellectual person, as is seen from his reference to his study under Gamaliel (Acts 22:3; Galatians 1:14), from his quoting Greek sources (Acts 17:28), and from the general depth of his reasoning. He certainly was not ignorant of the thought patterns and controversies of his day. But he wanted to get directly to the heart of this universal human need, which only the Lord Jesus Christ in his person and work could meet. Compared to this core area of truth, nothing else really mattered. Anything else that Paul could say would be secondary—actually unimportant compared to people's eternal destinies.

It is obvious that our Lord uses all kinds of people in his service, the uneducated as well as the educated, people of all backgrounds and social strata. It is interesting to observe, however, that two of the most prominent men in the Bible, men who had a very significant part in transmitting God's message in a definitive way, were men of extraordinary intellectual ability and superior educational attainments. These men are Moses in the Old Testament and Paul in the New Testament.

Stephen, in his historical address before the Sanhedrin, described Moses as "learned in all the wisdom of the Egyptians" (Acts 7:22). When God called Moses to lead the people of Israel out of Egypt, he did not cancel out all that Moses had learned during the first eighty years of his life. As the adopted son of pharaoh's daughter, Moses had many educational advantages. Even his years at the "back of the desert" (Exodus 3:1) taught him lessons which he used later in the service of God.

We have already noted Paul's educational attainments. Both Moses and Paul are outstanding examples of trained minds, each having undergone a long and arduous educational process. They are proof that spirituality and scholarship are not incompatible.

It should be an encouragement and a comfort to the weakest and least capable saint to know that even a great apostle had qualms about his proclamation of the gospel and people's acceptance of it. The weakness, fear, and trembling were not characteristics of cowardice, but the natural apprehension that accompanied this new and untried venture: preaching Christ and his death where he had never been even mentioned before.

Paul's words made it clear that God worked miracles to accompany his preaching. These were to validate and authenticate the message (Hebrews 2:1-4). God did not work miracles indiscriminately, but demonstrated in this way the "power" of the gospel.

THE TRUE WISDOM (2:6-13)

2:6 However, we speak wisdom among those who are mature, yet not the wisdom of this age, nor of the rulers of this age, who are coming to nothing.

2:7 But we speak the wisdom of God in a mystery, the hidden wisdom which God ordained before the ages for our glory,

2:8 which none of the rulers of this age knew; for had they known, they would not have crucified the Lord of glory.

2:9 But as it is written:

"Eye has not seen, nor ear heard,
Nor have entered into the heart of man
The things which God has prepared for those
who love Him."

2:10 But God has revealed them to us through His Spirit. For the Spirit searches all things, yes, the deep things of God.

2:11 For what man knows the things of a man except the spirit of the man which is in him? Even so no one knows the things of God except the Spirit of God.

2:12 Now we have received, not the spirit of the world, but the Spirit who is from God, that we might know the things that have been freely given to us by God.

2:13 These things we also speak, not in words which man's wisdom teaches but which the Holy Spirit teaches, comparing spiritual things with spiritual.

Note the emphasis all the way through this section on the two wisdoms: the wisdom of the world and the wisdom of God. The wisdom of the world is satanic in its origin, naturalistic in its method, and humanistic in its content.

The wisdom of God is divine in its origin, supernatural in its method, and Christ-centered in its content. The text declares that none of the rulers of this age knew this divine, hidden wisdom. In this passage, as well as in Peter's message at Solomon's porch (Acts 3:11), God reckons the most heinous sin of all time—the crucifixion of Christ—as a sin of ignorance (cf. Acts 3:17 and 1 Corinthians 2:8 with Luke 23:34).

Under the law, the sin and guilt offerings were only of value for the forgiveness of a sin committed "unintentionally" or in ignorance (Leviticus 4:2). This helps to explain David's exclamation in Psalm 51:16: "For You do not desire sacrifice, or else I would give it." There was no sacrifice in the levitical system that was sufficient for a deliberate sin. The only thing the sinner could do (and this is true in any dispensation) was to cast himself on God's mercy. By calling the crucifixion a sin of ignorance God is showing that even this can be forgiven.

Within this section Paul described two great doctrines which are basic to the Christian faith: the doctrine of revelation and the doctrine of inspiration. First he ruled out human methodology in discovering the "things of God."

That part of philosophy which encompasses the theory of knowledge is known technically as *epistemology*, from a Greek word meaning "to know" or "to be acquainted with." Many pessimistic philosophical systems have despaired of knowing anything. Others distrust even their knowledge of the natural world because they believe reality and their interpretation of that reality are radically different. "What is reality?" is the basic question asked in the area of philosophy known as *ontology*, the science of being. Sometimes the term *metaphysics is* used because of the position of this subject in Aristotle's treatises ("After the Physics"). Epistemology is closely related to the theory of reality because it asks questions such as "What can I know?" and "How do I know that I know?"

In the history of epistemology there have been two major approaches to knowledge. Many philosophers, both ancient and modern, have believed that the only valid knowledge is that which is gained through sensory experience—what can be seen, heard, touched, tasted or smelled. The designation most commonly given to this view is *empiricism*, "pertaining to experience."

The opposing school of epistemology is known as *rationalism*. This view says that the senses cannot be trusted, that our knowledge of the physical world is at best incomplete and imperfect

and at worst illusory. The senses, for example, show us a desk-
top, which seems to be a solid substance of some kind. Actually
the greatest part of it is empty space, and it consists of an
immense quantity of molecules, made up of atoms, which in turn
are made up of protons, neutrons, nuclei, etc., which are in fact
electrical energy of some kind and not "solid matter" at all.

The rationalist says that the only valid knowledge is that which
is achieved through the human reason on the basis of *a priori*
ideas, that is, self-evident propositions. Through reason alone
the rationalist claims to have an accurate picture of reality.

Many people, whether philosophers or not, believe that their
knowledge of the material world is gained partly through experience and partly through reason; in fact, that neither epistemo-
logical method is completely adequate, even in the everyday
experiences of life.

But when one comes to the "things of God," to spiritual reality,
scripture completely rules out both of these methods. God and
his works cannot be known through unaided experience ("Eye
has not seen nor ear heard") or through unaided reason ("nor
have entered into the heart of man"). How then can we know
these vital truths? Must we be like the existentialists, who
despair of knowing anything?

Thank God for the adversative conjunction *but!* "But God has
revealed them to us through His Spirit" (2:10). Revelation means
unveiling or disclosure; it is God's making known what otherwise
could never be known. Paul goes on to illustrate this in human
communication. One person may be able to guess what another
person is thinking, but he cannot really know unless the other
person tells him. Since that is so in human affairs where the
objects of knowledge and the knowers are on an equal plane,
how much more necessary it is if we are to know anything about
God. We cannot possibly know God's thoughts unless he tells
them to us. That telling is *revelation*.

Revelation was given to people called prophets, and this
included, among others, the writers of scripture (Hebrews 1:1).
Paul included himself among those who received direct revelations from God: "God has revealed them to us through His Spirit."

The next step is that the God-given revelation must be recorded
in permanent form. This is *inspiration*. "These things we also
speak, not in words which man's wisdom teaches but which the
Holy Spirit teaches." This is one of the major passages of the Bible

on the subject of verbal inspiration (see also 2 Timothy 3:15-17; 2 Samuel 23:2; 2 Peter 1:20-21). The Spirit-given message (revelation) is clothed in Spirit-given words (inspiration).

After the doctrine of the person and work of Christ, the area of theology most subject to the attacks of unbelieving critics is that of scripture (*bibliology*, or the doctrine of the Bible). Believing theologians have had to use a variety of terms to express the total teaching of the Bible itself on this subject. Hence we say that the Bible is a special divine revelation. That is, it originates with God himself (*theopneustos* or God-breathed); it is verbally inspired (the very words are from God); this inspiration is plenary (extending to all parts of the Bible); and the Bible is, therefore, infallible and inerrant (without error or mistakes of any kind). The one-sentence doctrinal statement of the Evangelical Theological Society expresses this well: "The Bible alone and the Bible in its entirety is the Word of God written, and is therefore inerrant in the autographs."

"NATURAL" OR "SPIRITUAL"? (2:14-16)

2:14 But the natural man does not receive the things of the Spirit of God, for they are foolishness to him; nor can he know them, because they are spiritually discerned.

2:15 But he who is spiritual judges all things, yet he himself is rightly judged by no one.

2:16 "For who has known the mind of the LORD that he may instruct Him?" But we have the mind of Christ.

There is still another step in the impartation of God's truth to mankind. God has made the disclosure (revelation); God has given the medium, the Spirit-given words (inspiration). But there still is a gap between God and man. Another ministry of the Spirit of God is required: *illumination*, or special enlightenment by the Holy Spirit.

In the section quoted above, the apostle demonstrated that there are three degrees of capacity for receiving and understanding these "things of God," which have been given by divine revelation and inspiration.

The first personal type discussed is the "natural man" (2:14). This adjective is related to the Greek word for "soul" (*psyche*). In this context it evidently refers to the unsaved person (NIV renders it "the man without the Spirit," which seems more of a paraphrase than a translation, although the rationale for it is probably Jude 19).

The natural man may have many praiseworthy qualities. He may even be a student of the Bible and may know a great many factual things about it. His capacity for receiving spiritual truth, however, is zero; he "does not receive the things of the Spirit of God." It is not that such a person is basically neutral; whatever he hears in spiritual matters he sooner or later labels as "foolishness." The Christian life is utterly beyond his comprehension.

The adverb *spiritually* here refers not to a quality of the perceiver but to the presence (or absence) of the Holy Spirit; they are by-the-Spirit discerned. The same Holy Spirit who gave the revelation by inspiration must give illumination to the human mind. Obviously he is not present in the natural man; therefore, that person has no capacity for receiving spiritual truth.

In contrast to the natural man is the spiritual man (2:15). This is a saved person who has yielded his life to God, opening the way for the Holy Spirit to work in him and through him. This epistle reveals the difference between possessing spiritual gifts (see especially chapter 12) and being spiritual (cf. 3:1). Spirituality involves yieldedness, followed by spiritual growth into maturity. This kind of yieldedness is described in Romans 6 and 12; note particularly the opening verses of chapter 12:

> I beseech you therefore, brethren, by the mercies of God, that you present your bodies a living sacrifice, holy, acceptable to God, which is your reasonable service. And do not be conformed to this world, but be transformed by the renewing of your mind, that you may prove what is that good and acceptable and perfect will of God.

The description of the spiritual person does not state or imply that such a person is perfect or that he understands all spiritual truth.What is indicated is that his capacity for accepting and assimilating spiritual truth is unlimited. He can grow and develop without hindrance. As the opposite of the natural person, who has no spiritual perception, the spiritual person has an ever-increasing perception. There are no boundaries to hem him in. His understanding knows no limits. The leading and empowering of the Holy Spirit, which equip him for this experience, give him extraordinary—in fact, supernatural—discernment (he "judges all things"). Furthermore, this person who is so widely and deeply discerning, is himself an enigma to the unsaved person; "he himself is rightly judged by no one." Nothing is more of a puzzle to the unsaved than the life of a Spirit-filled and Spirit-directed Christian.

The quotation in 2:16, from Isaiah 40:13, along with the statement, "But we have the mind of Christ," reminds us again of the believer's supernatural enablement.

THE CARNAL MAN (3:1-4)

3:1 And I, brethren, could not speak to you as to spiritual people but as to carnal, as to babes in Christ.

3:2 I fed you with milk and not with solid food; for until now you were not able to receive it, and even now you are still not able;

3:3 for you are still carnal. For where there are envy, strife, and divisions among you, are you not carnal and behaving like mere men?

3:4 For when one says, "I am of Paul," and another, "I am of Apollos," are you not carnal?

Most Christians recognize the distinction between saved and unsaved. But Paul showed that there is another category here when people are assessed according to their receptivity or non-receptivity of the word of God.

The natural man has no capacity for spiritual discernment; the spiritual man has unlimited capacity, which permits him to grow continually. But Paul informed us that in between is another group. The definitive word here is *carnal*. The adjective is formed from the noun *sarx*, which is usually translated "flesh." This word, however, has two different meanings in scripture. Sometimes it refers to the physical body or to physical existence, as in John 1:14 or 1 John 4:2-3 or Philippians 1:22-24.

The other usage of the word denotes the adamic nature, what the theologians call "original sin," as in Romans 8:9: "So then, those who are in the flesh cannot please God." In this last verse Paul quickly explained that in this sense the believer is "not in the flesh," though it is obvious that he is in his physical body.

The people in the third grouping in the immediate passage were not in the flesh either in that sense; nevertheless, they were described as "fleshly," "carnal." There are at least two evidences in the text that the ones described were saved people: Paul addressed them as "brethren" (3:1) and also designated them as "babes in Christ." They were babies, certainly, but not orphaned or alien babies; no, they were "babies in Christ."

Consequently, in between the natural man, an unsaved person with no capacity for receiving spiritual truth, and the spiritual man, who is a Christian with an unlimited and growing capacity for spiritual truth, is the carnal man, a Christian, but one whose capacity for spiritual truth is very limited.

Most people love babies; they are sweet and cute and adorable and lovable. But how tragic when a baby does not grow either physically or mentally. There is nothing wrong with being a spiritual infant if one is only newly born, but God wants his children to grow and develop into maturity. The apostle could not give those spiritual babies all that he would have liked. He could only keep on feeding them with the most elementary truths.

This is not the only place in scripture where such a contrast is drawn between milk and solid food. The writer of the epistle to the Hebrews uses the same figure:

> For everyone who partakes only of milk is unskilled in the word of righteousness, for he is a babe. But solid food belongs to those who are of full age, that is, those who by reason of use have their senses exercised to discern both good and evil (Hebrews 5:13-14).

People generally confine the word *carnal* to those kinds of sins that are thought of as grosser transgressions, particularly sexual sins. Note that although there were flagrant sexual sins in Corinth, yet when the apostle wanted to convince the believers of their carnality (fleshliness) he did not mention that type of sin, but instead reverted to the original complaint: that there were divisions among them.

"Are you not walking around according to man?" This is predictable human behavior, but God expects more of his children. Since their life was a supernatural one, their conduct ought to have been supernatural also.

At this point one can begin to see the relationship of the

lengthy discussion about the two wisdoms to the major point in the first four chapters of the epistle. That which caused the Corinthians to divide themselves in this tragic way was their adherence to the wisdom of the world instead of the wisdom of God. The true wisdom from God would unify them; the false wisdom of the world deeply divided them.

PARTNERSHIP OF GOD'S WORKERS (3:5-10)

3:5   Who then is Paul, and who is Apollos, but ministers through whom you believed, as the Lord gave to each one?

3:6   I planted, Apollos watered, but God gave the increase.

3:7   So then neither he who plants is anything, nor he who waters, but God who gives the increase.

3:8   Now he who plants and he who waters are one, and each one will receive his own reward according to his own labor.

3:9   For we are God's fellow workers; you are God's field, you are God's building.

3:10 According to the grace of God which was given to me, as a wise master builder I have laid the foundation, and another builds on it. But let each one take heed how he builds on it.

Paul turned the attention away from the individual human workers and focused it where it belongs: on God. Paul and Apollos and all the rest were mere "servants." Paul "planted"; that is, he was God's worker through whom they first heard the gospel and first believed. A little later Apollos came along and "watered," contributing to the growth of the tender plants. But the planter and the waterer, while important in God's program, are insignificant when compared to God. He himself is the one who gives the increase.

This does not mean that God would dispense with his servants. He gives them opportunity through which they minister to the eternal welfare of others and at the same time win for themselves a reward from him.

There is a sense in which God's workers are cooperating with him in accomplishing his purpose, but the particular thought in verse 9 is that we all belong to God as fellow workers with one another. Note the change of figure in verse 9 from workers to a "field" to a "building." Paul acknowledged that in regard to their salvation and development he "laid the foundation." He came among them in Corinth before anyone else had proclaimed the good news to them. They had never heard of Christ. Hence the pervasive emphasis in this section about their unique relationship to Paul and his to them (cf. 4:15).

There seems to be a blending here of one idea with another. Paul and those who followed him had the obligation to build on the one foundation alone, and that foundation is Jesus Christ. A closely related idea was introduced, seeming to refer to the individual Christian's building his life and service.

BUILDING ON THE FOUNDATION (3:11-15)

3:11 For no other foundation can anyone lay than that which is laid, which is Jesus Christ.

3:12 Now if anyone builds on this foundation with gold, silver, precious stones, wood, hay, straw,

3:13 each one's work will become clear; for the Day will declare it, because it will be revealed by fire; and the fire will test each one's work, of what sort it is.

3:14 If anyone's work which he has built on it endures, he will receive a reward.

3:15 If anyone's work is burned, he will suffer loss; but he himself will be saved, yet so as through fire.

That the apostle was not speaking of salvation is clear in the context. Parallels are found in 2 Corinthians 5:1-10 and in Romans 14:8-12. In all of these passages the subject of rewards is in view. Decisive words which make this clear are *work* (1 Corinthians 3:13-15) and *reward* (3:14). Consequently, the "loss" mentioned in 3:15 could not possibly be loss of salvation, but must be loss of reward. In fact, the very next clause after the one that pronounces "loss" says plainly, "But he himself will be saved, yet so as through fire."

The passage does not speak of quantity or amount of work, but of quality or kind of work. It is not always possible for us to label other people's work accurately as either "gold" or "straw," but we can judge in a general way without questioning the motives of other people's hearts what kind of work or service is lasting and what is not. To spend one's life in laziness and self-indulgence is certainly not the will of the Lord Jesus. The admonition of 1 John 2:28 is very important: "And now, little children, abide in Him, that when He appears, we may have confidence and not be ashamed before Him at His coming."

One lesson we Christians can learn from unbelievers who are dedicated to some earthly task is one of intense concentration on what we are doing. Paul in other places used athletic preparation and attainment as figurative for the kind of earnestness the Christian should put into his life (cf. 9:24-27). The unbeliever often will show admirable qualities of perseverance and intense dedication to an ephemeral task, while the Christian often demonstrates a lackadaisical attitude toward the most important eternal values (cf. 1 Corinthians 9:24-27; Philippians 3:12-14).

A person would not continue consulting a medical doctor who knows nothing of physiology and anatomy. Similarly, one would avoid a pharmacist whose knowledge of drugs and medicines is incomplete and questionable. If one needs a lawyer as defense counsel in meeting a serious charge, it is not likely he would turn to someone whose knowledge of the law is hazy and inadequate. Should not Christians be at their best and do their best—for the Lord and not for self? One who aspires to Christian leadership must prepare and equip himself for it.

THE CHURCH, THE TEMPLE OF GOD (3:16-17)

> 3:16 Do you not know that you are the temple of God and that the Spirit of God dwells in you?
>
> 3:17 If anyone defiles the temple of God, God will destroy him. For the temple of God is holy, which temple you are.

A temple is a dwelling place of God, a sanctuary where God meets his worshiping people. In the Old Testament era Israel, the people of God, had a temple, a building of wood and stone, embellished and emblazoned with gold, silver, and many kinds of precious gems. The temple which Solomon built is described at length and designated as "magnificent" (1 Chronicles 22:5). In contrast, the church, the people of God in the New Testament, *is* a temple (note Ephesians 2:19-22; 1 Peter 2:4-5).

In this passage the church collectively is called a temple (the pronoun is plural in the Greek). Later (6:19) Paul developed a related truth that the body of each individual believer in Christ is a temple of the Holy Spirit.

The solemn warning to anyone who would seek to do harm to the "temple of God" makes it plain that an attack against the true church is regarded by God as an attack against himself (cf. Hebrews 12:29).

ALL THINGS OURS (3:18-23)

3:18 Let no one deceive himself. If anyone among you seems to be wise in this age, let him become a fool that he may become wise.

3:19 For the wisdom of this world is foolishness with God. For it is written, "He catches the wise in their own craftiness";

3:20 and again, "The LORD knows the thoughts of the wise, that they are futile."

3:21 Therefore let no one boast in men. For all things are yours:

3:22 whether Paul or Apollos or Cephas, or the world or life or death, or things present or things to come—all are yours.

3:23 And you are Christ's, and Christ is God's.

Ultimately each individual must choose for himself which "wisdom" he is going to adopt and follow. To adopt the wisdom of this world leads to destruction. True wisdom includes the capacity for being willing to be thought a fool. Each of these spheres is antithetical to the other. The most elaborately conceived display of what the world considers wisdom is, in the final analysis, empty and "futile." This is the conclusion reached by Solomon in Ecclesiastes after he had tried the various forms and methods of human philosophy. Life lived only and completely on the earthly plane, "under the sun," is meaningless. "Vanity of vanities, all is vanity" (Ecclesiastes 1:2).

To "boast in men," that is, to boast about human leaders, is not only wrong but also unnecessary. What can any human being add to the possessions that we have in Christ? Because of our association with him, we possess the universe. Selfish possession, in which one believes that he holds on personally to some part of God's universe, is meaningless, for he had none of it to begin with, and even what he seems to have will be taken away from him. Belonging to Christ, who is the heir, assures one of active participation in the whole universe forever and ever. Paul, Apollos, and Cephas are thus seen to be not heads of disparate parties but channels leading to the fullness of the Lord Jesus Christ, who is himself God.

REQUIREMENT OF STEWARDS (4:1-5)

4:1 Let a man so consider us, as servants of Christ and stewards of the mysteries of God.
4:2 Moreover it is required in stewards that one be found faithful.
4:3 But with me it is a very small thing that I should be judged by you or by a human court. In fact I do not even judge myself.
4:4 For I know of nothing against myself, yet I am not justified by this; but He who judges me is the Lord.
4:5 Therefore judge nothing before the time, until the Lord comes, who will both bring to light the hidden things of darkness and reveal the counsels of the hearts. Then each one's praise will come from God.

Several Greek words are translated "servants" in our most widely used English versions. This one (4:1) means literally "underrowers," referring to those oarsmen in a large Roman galley or fighting ship who handle the lowest bank of oars under the emphatic rhythm of the overseer. The idea behind the word seems to evoke the necessity of this type of worker, but at the same time his individual littleness within the whole company of workers. This same word is used in Acts 13:5 of John Mark (NKJV, "assistant").

Along with the term *servants* is another significant word, *stewards*. A steward is literally a "household manager" (*oikonomos*), one who administers affairs or manages property belonging to someone else. The sphere of management in this case is not earthly property, but "the mysteries of God." The Greek word *mysterion* ("secret") is used in a technical sense in the New Testament for something not clearly revealed by God in the Old Testament, which has now been plainly disclosed in the New

Testament. The secret things belonging to God were in sharp contrast to the so-called mystery religions of the Greco-Roman world in Paul's day. It is a serious enough business to be a steward or agent of someone's earthly property. How much more important it is, and how much more sobering, to be a steward of secret things belonging to God.

No doubt a steward might require many qualities, such as special talents, acquired abilities, depth of experience, etc., but none of these would really matter if the steward were disloyal to his master's person or interests. Faithfulness is the *sine qua non* for effective and successful stewardship. Since Paul wanted the Corinthians to judge himself and God's other servants on this basis, it was necessary that he and they maintain that unswerving dedication to God's property which can be recognized and acknowledged by all observers.

Nevertheless, Paul did not by any means accept the Corinthians' judgments or those of any other human beings as final or definitive. Human judges, even the most well-intentioned, are likely to be mistaken in many of their conclusions. This was the reason that Paul, putting all things in a heavenly perspective, considered their judgment a "very small thing" in the light of God's eternity. The expression, "by a human court" (NKJV, NASB, NIV), seems somewhat clumsy. The KJV, "man's judgment," is more felicitous in the light of the original, which is literally "man's day." This appears to be in contrast to God's day, the "day of the LORD," which is used repeatedly by some of the Old Testament prophets to describe the future intervention of God in direct judgment on the world. Man now seems to be in control—although not really so—but the time is coming when God will be recognizably in control. The believing and obedient child of God can afford to wait, difficult as that sometimes seems, for the final verdict from the completely righteous judge. In view of that prospect, Paul and others like him could be content to hear the opinions of "man's day" without being unduly disturbed.

In fact, the apostle said he did not even trust his own judgment about himself. There were so many unknown factors that one could not even decipher all one's own thoughts, much less those of others. Paul rested his case before the supreme court, being willing to await that outcome, because he was fully aware that the Lord Jesus Christ—his judge—is omniscient, omnipotent, and absolutely righteous in all that he says and does.

Paul's advice then to the Corinthians was that they learn his secret of reserving judgment, of being willing to let some things remain undecided until the appropriate time. The Lord's judgment has been alluded to in chapter 3. We have the intimation there and elsewhere in scripture that the Lord Jesus Christ, being infinite, as one of the persons of the Godhead, can give infinite and undivided attention to each individual at the same time as he is doing the same thing for every other individual. This event is described in 2 Corinthians 5:10 as being manifested before "the judgment seat [bema] of Christ." In the ruins of the marketplace of ancient Corinth is a raised platform that was the bema, the place of judgment, before which Paul and other believers stood. How different a judge will the Lord Jesus Christ be from Gallio and all other officials of "man's day"!

Is it not a comforting thought—although it may in another sense be terrifying—to know that judgment is in the control of the savior who died for us? There is a time of judgment coming, no matter how long it seems to be delayed or how much sneered at by unbelieving "scoffers" (2 Peter 3:3-4).

Some have interpreted the last clause in verse 5 to mean that the Lord Jesus will find something in even the weakest and least productive saint to praise or mention favorably. It is true, certainly, that God saves us by his grace, entirely apart from works, then enables us by his grace to live for him, and then rewards us for what his grace has enabled us to do. Whatever praise comes to the believer at the judgment seat of Christ will come from God, not from man, and will therefore be genuine and meaningful. God can be fully trusted to render absolutely right judgments. This verse brings out those factors that are invariably hidden or unknown in our present condition: "the hidden things of darkness" and "the counsels of the hearts." It is no wonder that the Lord admonished his disciples and all of us, "Judge not that you be not judged" (Matthew 7:1). How could any of us know another's heart well enough to render a correct judgment?

We must note, however, that judgment forbidden by the Lord Jesus Christ is not the same as expressing oneself on conduct of others which is directly and palpably contrary to the written word of God. That is not only not forbidden, but actually enjoined on the church, as chapter 5 clearly reveals (1 Corinthians 5:3).

To judge a confessed murderer as a murderer is not forbidden judgment in this or any dispensation. Furthermore, we must distinguish between overt factual knowledge of disobedience to, or failure to live up to, scripture and drawing unwarranted conclusions about someone from our own unaided observation or reasoning.

PAUL'S APPROPRIATE IRONY (4:6-13)

4:6 Now these things, brethren, I have figuratively transferred to myself and Apollos for your sakes, that you may learn in us not to think beyond what is written, that none of you may be puffed up on behalf of one against the other.

4:7 For who makes you differ from another? And what do you have that you did not receive? Now if you did indeed receive it, why do you boast as if you had not received it?

4:8 You are already full! You are already rich! You have reigned as kings without us—and indeed I could wish you did reign, that we also might reign with you!

4:9 For I think that God has displayed us, the apostles, last, as men condemned to death; for we have been made a spectacle to the world, both to angels and to men.

4:10 We are fools for Christ's sake, but you are wise in Christ! We are weak, but you are strong! You are distinguished, but we are dishonored!

4:11 To the present hour we both hunger and thirst, and we are poorly clothed, and beaten, and homeless.

4:12 And we labor, working with our own hands. Being reviled, we bless; being persecuted, we endure;

4:13 being defamed, we entreat. We have been made as the filth of the world, the offscouring of all things until now.

In verse 6 Paul stated that he and Apollos were not literally the problem for the Corinthians. He had used the eloquent Alexandrian and himself as possible examples of human leaders who might have been innocently maligned and misused by those who were favoring factionalism in the church.

The apostle has shown conclusively that no one should be put up as the head of a faction in the church, much less of the whole church. By observing the examples of Paul and Apollos in their extreme care not to offend in this way, the Corinthians could learn a lesson about their own attitudes. It would be difficult to create a faction if the proposed head or leader absolutely refused to be identified with it. Since the proposed leaders refused to be "puffed up," their self-appointed followers had no grounds for getting puffed up either, as if one group were better than another within the body of Christ.

Verse 7 demonstrates the complete folly of thinking oneself better than others. None of us had anything to do personally with our inborn traits; how could we justifiably be proud of them? Tracing everything we have back to its source, we must conclude that we do not have anything inherent in ourselves; everything we have can be traced back to its original source: God himself. Where is there then any ground for boasting?

The Puritan commentator Matthew Henry spoke of four kinds of pride among men and even among Christians, all of them reprehensible: pride of race, pride of place, pride of face, and pride of grace.

It seems obvious that the last of these must surely be the worst of all. How can one be proud of something that is entirely a free gift of God, undeserved, unearned, and unrecompensed? The Corinthians were indeed guilty of this climactic kind of pride. Paul therefore chided them and did not refrain from a well-deserved sarcasm. "You are already full!"

The Corinthians apparently were confusing their dispensations.They were neglecting their responsibilities to live for Christ now in this world, which involved suffering and persecution, and they were acting as though the millennial kingdom had already begun and the Lord Jesus had already apportioned his rewards. They were proud and boastful.

In contrast, Paul said that he and the other apostles were enduring suffering and hardship in this world for Christ's sake. In the listing of verse 10 there are both simple fact and irony. The apostles were willing to be "fools for Christ's sake." Again we must recognize how Paul used the term. They were not actually fools in God's sight, but were regarded as fools when judged according to the "wisdom of this world." They not only were willing but even happy to be considered fools by that standard. The Corinthians, on the other hand, professed to be wise, while really making fools of themselves when judged in the light of God's day. The evidence of this folly was furnished by the strife and division within the church. Only as God's children assume their rightful stance before the world will they honor and glorify him in and through their lives.

The word *spectacle* (4:9) is the Greek *theatron*. From this comes the word *theater*. Paul and the other apostles were being intently observed by those around them. People were wondering how they would act and react to the circumstances, which were far from favorable.Perhaps you have heard the story of the man who walked about carrying a sign front and back. He may not have had the greatest method, but he hit the point of this teaching. On his chest the sign read, "A fool for Christ's sake." The other sign, on his back, asked, "Whose fool are you?" The Corinthians, while claiming to be wise, were following the wrong standard. This was manifested, as we have seen, in the unconscionable quarreling within the church.

PAUL'S FATHERLY WARNING (4:14-21)

4:14 I do not write these things to shame you, but as my beloved children I warn you.
4:15 For though you might have ten thousand instructors in Christ, yet you do not have many fathers; for in Christ Jesus I have begotten you through the gospel.
4:16 Therefore I urge you, imitate me.
4:17 For this reason I have sent Timothy to you, who is my beloved and faithful son in the Lord, who will remind you of my ways in Christ, as I teach everywhere in every church.
4:18 Now some are puffed up, as though I were not coming to you.
4:19 But I will come to you shortly, if the Lord wills, and I will know, not the word of those who are puffed up, but the power.
4:20 For the kingdom of God is not in word but in power.
4:21 What do you want? Shall I come to you with a rod, or in love and a spirit of gentleness?

Again the fervent love of the apostle is seen in the way in which he wrote of things that must have been painful to them as well as to him. He had a legitimate claim on them and he let them know it. He was their spiritual father.

In many instances the command, "Imitate me," might have

been taken as utter presumption, but Paul was able to say this without boastfulness or effrontery, for in his life he imitated the Lord Jesus Christ, as he was careful to mention later (11:1).

Timothy was seen as a worthy example of Paul's children; the Corinthians could learn from him how they should act toward their spiritual father Paul. In sending Timothy Paul showed the importance of personal testimony along with formal written instructions. Timothy, because of long and close association with Paul, was well qualified to remind them of Paul's "ways in Christ."

The text makes it obvious that there were some persons in the Corinthian church who were seeking to seize the leadership of the congregation. Paul never named these people in either of the Corinthian epistles, but they clearly were fostering the party spirit and were probably in the fourth group ("of Christ"). A part of their pretensions evidently included a derogation of Paul's authority and—as seen in the second epistle—a denigration of his person and character (2 Corinthians 10:1-6). They may even have been boasting that Paul would not return to Corinth because he was afraid of them.

Paul's certain coming would reveal the falsity of the pretensions of these men. As an apostle, Paul had been given certain authority by God, which included the power to discipline those who were living and teaching in ways contrary to God's commands. But he did not want to come as a stern disciplinarian. He very much wanted the problems to be settled before he came so that he could come among them as a gentle and loving father, friend, or brother.

With his questions at the end of chapter 4, Paul brought to a close his treatment of the first problem in the epistle: the problem of divisions. But other very serious problems remained, reminding us that this was a "problem church." God, however, through his servant, had the solution to the problems.

PROBLEM TWO

Discipline
1 Corinthians 5–6

THE CASE OF THE IMMORAL CHURCH MEMBER (5:1-8)

5:1 It is actually reported that there is sexual immorality among you, and such sexual immorality as is not even named among the Gentiles—that a man has his father's wife!

5:2 And you are puffed up, and have not rather mourned, that he who has done this deed might be taken away from among you.

5:3 For I indeed, as absent in body but present in spirit, have already judged (as though I were present) him who has so done this deed.

5:4 In the name of our Lord Jesus Christ, when you are gathered together, along with my spirit, with the power of our Lord Jesus Christ,

5:5 deliver such a one to Satan for the destruction of the flesh, that his spirit may be saved in the day of the Lord Jesus.

5:6 Your glorying is not good. Do you not know that a little leaven leavens the whole lump?

5:7 Therefore purge out the old leaven, that you may be a new lump, since you truly are unleavened. For indeed Christ, our Passover, was sacrificed for us.

5:8 Therefore let us keep the feast, not with old leaven, nor with the leaven of malice and wickedness, but with the unleavened bread of sincerity and truth.

The account of the incestuous man seems to have been the second major problem related to Paul in Ephesus by those of Chloe's household. Here was a vital matter requiring consistent and emphatic church discipline.

We have already seen that Corinth was notorious for immoral behavior of many kinds. This example, however, outpaganed the pagans ("not even named among the Gentiles")! Roman law forbade this kind of union. Yet some in the church not only were tolerating this immoral behavior, but were proud of their supposed broad-mindedness in tolerating it.

One of the perversions of the gospel is the false idea that because salvation is by grace the Christian may live as he pleases without regard to the will of God. Paul considered this general proposition in Romans:

> What shall we say then? Shall we continue in sin that grace may abound? Certainly not! How shall we who died to sin live any longer in it? (Romans 6:1-2).

God's grace is not a license to sin. Salvation is *from* sin, not *to* sin.

Most interpreters believe that the woman in question was not the offender's mother, but his stepmother. The form of expression, "his father's wife," seems to support this view.

Part of the apathy of the church was no doubt because of their wrong ideas about grace and about the Christian life. Another part may have come from a misunderstanding of the words of the Lord Jesus in his sermon on the mount: "Judge not that you be not judged" (Matthew 7:1). This has been dealt with above. To recognize that this man was living immorally did not involve the kind of judgment the Lord Jesus was talking about. Any decision about the case was not based at all on an individual's inner conviction or supposition, but on the actual fact of behavior and the plain teaching of scripture.

This section introduces a subject often neglected in the church today: church discipline, including the necessity on occasion of excommunication or official solemn judicial removal of an unrepentant sinner from the fellowship of the church. The Lord Jesus laid down the usual procedure (Matthew 18:15-17). The attitude of those making this serious judgment should be that described in Galatians 6:1:

> Brethren, if a man is overtaken in any trespass, you
> who are spiritual restore such a one in a spirit of gen-
> tleness, considering yourself lest you also be tempted.

In the easygoing toleration of the professing church of today
Paul might be dismissed with the scornful epithet,
"Judgmental!" But we have to be judgmental in this sense, for
action requires sober judgment based on a thorough knowledge of the word of God.

The prescribed procedure no doubt indicates that this man
had been dealt with, that he had been urged to stop his
immoral behavior, and that he not only refused to do so but
probably was claiming the sanction of God's grace to excuse
the inexcusable. All kinds of unscriptural moves are suggested in such cases. "Oh, don't be so hard on this poor man!
After all, we are all sinners. We all make mistakes, and we all
are saved by the grace of God, not by our works." The passages from Matthew and Galatians take care of these cavils, if
carefully read and properly interpreted.

The meaning of "deliver such a one to Satan for the destruction of the flesh" is unclear; this is perhaps the greatest difficulty in the passage. Very likely it means carefully and
solemnly to put this unrepentant professed Christian out of
the sphere of the church (the people of God) back into Satan's
realm (the world) from which he had come. It is possible that
there is an allusion to Job here also:

> So the LORD said to Satan, "Behold, all that he has is in
> your power; only do not lay a hand on his person" (Job
> 1:12).
>
> So the LORD said to Satan, "Behold, he is in your hand,
> but spare his life" (Job 2:6).

The teaching is clear in Job that Satan could not afflict Job
without God's permission. There seems to be an implication
in the present passage that the formal action of the church
would, in some way, be exposing the immoral person to
Satan's attacks.

But what is the meaning here of the expression "destruction
of the flesh"? Is it a reference to the adamic nature? It is
hardly likely that this procedure could "destroy" that.
Probably the word *flesh* is used for the body, as in numerous

other scripture passages. In permitting Satan to afflict the man in some way, there may be an indication that such trouble would help to drive the man to repentance and forsaking of his sin. Obviously his case is not parallel to Job's situation because God plainly said that Satan had moved him against Job "without cause" (Job 2:3). There was more than sufficient cause in the life of the immoral man.

It is possible that the offender described in 2 Corinthians is this same man, now repentant. There Paul's decision was to restore him (2 Corinthians 2:6-7). God treats the repentant sinner differently than he does the unrepentant sinner, not because of any change in God, who is unchangeable, but because of a decided change in the individual.

The Corinthians, boasting about their tolerance, were probably reasoning that by overlooking the man's faults they could love him into a change of behavior. The apostle's dictum was just the opposite. First, the church must do what is right (and that is clearly determined from scripture) regardless of what that does to the person, leaving the outcome in God's hands. The possible result, however, may be that the discipline—the hard, sad process of excommunication—will bring him back to God in a way that accepting or ignoring his confirmed sinfulness will not.

"That his spirit may be saved . . . " By these words Paul expressed his faith that God will act when the church does what is right, and that this seemingly harsh treatment may turn out for the sinner's eternal welfare. Like the prodigal son, the man may indeed come "to himself" (Luke 15:17).

In 1 Corinthians 5:6 Paul used what was probably a well-known saying in his day: "A little leaven leavens the whole lump." Here it describes the spread of wrong conduct among the body of believers through the example of one who persists in wrongdoing. The apostle quoted the same proverb in Galatians 5:9 to demonstrate the spread of false doctrine within the church.

In commanding the believers to "purge out the old leaven" Paul gave the meaning of the Old Testament Passover and the feast of unleavened bread. "For indeed Christ our Passover, was sacrificed for us" (1 Corinthians 5:7). Every lamb killed, from the first observance of this ordinance in Egypt in Moses' day all through the centuries, was pointing to the "Lamb of

God who takes away the sin of the world" (John 1:29). Just as the blood applied to the doorposts of the Israelites' houses guaranteed the safety of the firstborn within, so the blood of Christ shed on Calvary's cross guarantees the eternal salvation of everyone who trusts in him.

As the Passover prefigured our salvation, so the feast of unleavened bread points toward the life resulting from that salvation. Known sin unjudged hinders God's working in and through the church. Leaven is seen here, as in other passages of scripture, as symbolic of sin—not that there is anything inherently sinful about the leavening agent, whether it be yeast or something else, but that its rapid and total spread symbolizes the working of sin within an individual or within the whole assembly of believers.

EXPLANATION OF PAUL'S COMMAND (5:9-13)

5:9   I wrote to you in my epistle not to keep company with sexually immoral people.

5:10 Yet I certainly did not mean with the sexually immoral people of this world, or with the covetous, or extortioners, or idolaters, since then you would need to go out of the world.

5:11 But now I have written to you not to keep company with anyone named a brother, who is sexually immoral, or covetous, or an idolater, or a reviler, or a drunkard, or an extortioner—not even to eat with such a person.

5:12 For what have I to do with judging those also who are outside? Do you not judge those who are inside?

5:13 But those who are outside God judges. Therefore, "put away from yourselves the evil person."

Verse 9 introduces the question of how many letters Paul wrote to the Corinthians. Most commentators apparently believe that he wrote four, only two of which have been preserved. Several questions must be faced. Did Paul and the other writers of the New Testament epistles write other letters? It seems unlikely that in a ministry of twenty-five or thirty years Paul would have written only thirteen letters.

One possible indication of an otherwise unknown letter may be the reference to the "epistle from Laodicea" (Colossians 4:16). This may mean a letter to Laodicea from Paul, which was then to be sent from Laodicea to Colosse, so that the believers in the latter church could have been helped by it. Some believe, however, that this was actually the letter that we know as Ephesians, since the words *en Epheso* are not in Codex B and Codex Aleph. In refutation of this see Burgon, *The Revision Revised*, page 317 and *passim*.

It is very probable that Paul wrote other letters in the course of his long ministry, but that it was not the purpose of God to include all of these in the written word. Would this mean then that the non-extant letters were not inspired? Not necessarily. The Old Testament prophets often delivered oral messages from God (as attested by the words, "Thus says the LORD"). Such messages were direct revelations from God, inspired by the Holy Spirit, but not intended to be part of the permanent written revelation. The proper distinction should be not between inspired and uninspired, but between canonical and non-canonical.

According to the most widely held view about the Corinthian epistles, Paul wrote a letter prior to 1 Corinthians, to which he alludes in the present passage (5:9). Our canonical 1 Corinthians, then, is the second letter to that congregation. After sending 1 Corinthians, Paul supposedly wrote a third letter, to which he refers in 2 Corinthians 2:4, and which is often designated by commentators as "the severe letter." Consequently, our canonical 2 Corinthians would be, according to this view, the fourth letter from Paul to this church.

There does not seem to be any serious difficulty in accepting such a view, for scripture on other occasions refers to letters or earlier books, which in God's providence have not been preserved. These could not be called "lost books" of the Bible because God never intended that they should be in the Bible.

Another possibility, however, may be that in 1 Corinthians 5:9 Paul was simply using the epistolary aorist and consequently was referring in this place to what he had just written. This could be translated: "I am writing to you in my epistle . . ." NKJV, NASB, and NIV all seem at least to allow for this possibility by translating "my letter" instead of "a letter" (KJV, "an epistle"), a truly commendable avoidance of interpretation (for translators, not commentators) in a place of such uncertainty. The reference by Clement of Rome in his epistle to the Corinthians, about A.D. 100, seems clearly to be to the canonical 1 Corinthians.

One would think it obvious that the Christian could not completely avoid contacts with immoral unsaved people. "You would need to go out of the world," Paul exclaimed. Furthermore, to do that would be to abandon that task which the Lord Jesus himself made the most important: to be witnesses to the ends of the earth (Acts 1:8).

Scripture does not forbid the association of Christians with unsaved people. The Lord Jesus himself was accused of being a sinner because he "ate with tax collectors and sinners." He emphasized, in replying to men's accusations, that he had come not "to call the righteous, but sinners to repentance" (Luke 5:32). Carrying on ordinary business dealings with the unsaved will not compromise the testimony; in fact, it may give occasion to enhance the testimony and even to win some to Christ.

Fellowship with a professing Christian, however, who is living contrary to scripture is another matter, as verse 11 emphatically declares. Paul did not confine his remarks to one sin or one kind of sin. Immorality is mentioned prominently, since that was the occasion of these instructions, but a "covetous" person and a "reviler" are included in the list.

There is obviously an obligation on the part of the assembly to require scriptural standards of conduct from its members. This area is often neglected in the church today. The final command in the paragraph is quoted from Deuteronomy 17:7; 19:19; 22:21-24; and 24:7. In the Old Testament it involved judicial execution: the penalty of death. Here, although it is a sentence of excommunication rather than execution, it must be treated very carefully and solemnly. The church dare not overlook or disobey these instructions. Yet how sad it is that so many churches, even some evangelical ones, neglect or refuse to exercise discipline over members who are flagrantly disobeying the word of God. This is detrimental to the spiritual growth of any congregation. The apostle John penned a similar warning for those who mistakenly suppose they are to tolerate false teachers:

> If anyone comes to you and does not bring this doctrine, do not receive him into your house nor greet him; for he who greets him shares in his evil deeds (2 John 10-11).

LAWSUITS AMONG BELIEVERS (6:1-8)

6:1 Dare any of you, having a matter against another, go to law before the unrighteous and not before the saints?

6:2 Do you not know that the saints will judge the world? And if the world will be judged by you, are you unworthy to judge the smallest matters?

6:3 Do you not know that we shall judge angels? How much more, things that pertain to this life?

6:4 If then you have judgments concerning things pertaining to this life, do you appoint those who are least esteemed by the church to judge?

6:5 I say this to your shame. Is it so, that there is not a wise man among you, not even one, who will be able to judge between his brethren?

6:6 But brother goes to law against brother, and that before unbelievers!

6:7 Now therefore, it is already an utter failure for you that you go to law against one another. Why do you not rather accept wrong? Why do you not rather let yourselves be cheated?

6:8 No, you yourselves do wrong and cheat, and you do these things to your brethren!

The instructions about lawsuits may properly be included in the section on discipline because of its damaging effect on the testimony of the local church.

These instructions do not condemn all uses of law courts by Christians. Paul himself made full use of the Roman law and its courts when he was accused of crime and wrongdoing. Rather than surrender to the unreasoning hatred of his Jewish accusers, he appealed to Caesar, the highest right of a Roman citizen (Acts 25:10-11). All of the judicial processes of the great empire were thus set in motion to take Paul to Rome.

The situation in Corinth seems to have been a proliferation of petty quarrels among Christians, which led to numerous and unnecessary uses of the judicial process. One of the end results, of course, was to bring the quarreling Christians into disrepute with their pagan neighbors. Furthermore, what did the unsaved judges know about the relationships of Christians with one another? How could they then judge cases wisely and accurately?

Some years earlier, during Paul's time in Corinth, the proconsul Gallio had sense enough to recognize this and would not adjudicate in an accusation brought by unbelieving Jews against the Christians (Acts 18:14-17). The Roman magistrates certainly would not have been aware of the finer points of what they would have considered religious quarrels.

In warning against these procedures Paul alluded to the fact that Christians are to have a part in judging the world, and he mentioned our judging angels. Several passages inform us that the fallen angels are awaiting judgment (Jude 6; 2 Peter 2:4), but this is apparently the only passage in which we are told specifically that *we* shall judge angels. Scripture is silent on the details, but it is an earnest and solemn duty that awaits us. The point seems to be that we should learn by experience and "get in practice" for these more demanding judgments by helping now to settle disputes among fellow believers. Our appointed destiny suggests that we have more capability for judging present cases and solving present problems than we might have thought.

Verse 4 is one of the more difficult parts of this section. It could mean that for relatively small matters pertaining to this life we can entrust the judgment to those of lesser repute in the church, in view of the coming responsibility we shall all bear.

Another possibility is that the words form a question (as in NKJV) and that the members of the pagan legal system are those "least esteemed by the church." According to this view, even a weak and poorly equipped saint is more capable of making a right judgment than the most knowledgeable unbelieving judge.

The Sanctity of the Body (6:9-20)

6:9   Do you not know that the unrighteous will not inherit the kingdom of God? Do not be deceived. Neither fornicators, nor idolaters, nor adulterers, nor homosexuals, nor sodomites,

6:10 nor thieves, nor covetous, nor drunkards, nor revilers, nor extortioners will inherit the kingdom of God.

6:11 And such were some of you. But you were washed, but you were sanctified, but you were justified in the name of the Lord Jesus and by the Spirit of our God.

6:12 All things are lawful for me, but all things are not helpful.   All things are lawful for me, but I will not be brought under the power of any.

6:13 Foods for the stomach and the stomach for foods, but God will destroy both it and them. Now the body is not for sexual immorality but for the Lord, and the Lord for the body.

6:14 And God both raised up the Lord and will also raise us up by His power.

6:15 Do you not know that your bodies are members of Christ? Shall I then take the members of Christ and make them members of a harlot? Certainly not!

6:16 Or do you not know that he who is joined to a harlot is one body with her? For "the two," He says, "shall become one flesh."

6:17 But he who is joined to the Lord is one spirit with Him.

6:18 Flee sexual immorality. Every sin that a man does is outside the body, but he who commits sexual immorality sins against his own body.

6:19 Or do you not know that your body is the temple of the Holy Spirit who is in you, whom you have from God, and you are not your own?

6:20 For you were bought at a price; therefore glorify God in your body and in your spirit, which are God's.

The consideration of what the Corinthians should have done about legal difficulties led back to a previous subject and enabled the apostle to develop more fully the truth of the sanctity or holiness of the human body as contrasted with the prevalent immorality in the surrounding culture. The mention of judging the world and angels was logically connected with the coming kingdom of God. But who are to live and reign in that future blessed realm? The Lord Jesus had made it clear to Nicodemus that only through a new birth from above could anyone enter God's kingdom. The thought here in Corinthians is parallel to the words of the Lord Jesus—not that participation in the kingdom is by works or that anyone who has ever committed any of the sins mentioned here is forever barred from the kingdom.

Paul instead described the settled manner of life of people who are not to have a part in the kingdom. He first used the most general term for any and every kind of sexual immorality (*porneia*), usually translated in the KJV as "fornication," referring to those involved in such misconduct (*pornoi*), translated in KJV and in NKJV as "fornicators," meaning those who practice any kind of sexual immorality. Idolaters were then mentioned, probably because of the association of idolatry with sexual immorality in the Old Testament and in the practice of the pagan Greeks.

The next term, *adulterers* (*moichoi*), is almost synonymous with the first word, but is normally used to designate sexual immorality which involves unfaithfulness in an existing marriage relationship.

Two terms were then used to describe homosexual relationships.The first, *malakoi*, is translated in NKJV as "homosexuals" with the footnote, "That is, catamites." The old KJV uses the word "effeminate," which tries to convey that in a male homosexual relationship this is the partner who takes the place filled by the female in a heterosexual union. This is the precise meaning of the word *catamite*. The other corresponding term is then *sodomite*, for which see Genesis 19. In the culture of our day, which recognizes no final accountability for any of one's actions, there is widespread acceptance of those types of behavior that God's word condemns. This is taught in a parallel passage in Romans, in which men are seen as given up by

God, permitted to persist in their sinfulness even though they will ultimately come under his severe judgment (Romans 1:18-32). The concluding verse in that passage summarizes the tragic prospect: "Who, knowing the righteous judgment of God, that those who practice such things are deserving of death, not only do the same but also approve of those who practice them" (Romans 1:32).

Like the ancient Corinthians, we are living in a cultural environment in which there is not only toleration but actually applause for every kind of flagrant sin. Homosexuals in particular are flaunting their beliefs and actions with a perversity that would have been considered intolerable a generation, or even a decade, ago. Newspapers, magazines, television, radio, and films are using words and supporting or condoning conduct that is plainly declared in scripture to be under the righteous judgment of God.

The outstanding fact of verse 11 is the past tense of the verb: "Such *were* some of you." Christ delivered them from the terrible shackles of the past. H. A. Ironside's comment is, as usual, appropriate and practical:

> And then think of what grace has already done for you. Think of how marvelously God has dealt with you in spite of all the sin and iniquity that you have been guilty of in the past. . . . You are sinners of five hundred pence, but God has forgiven all. Shall you hold your brother accountable because he owes you a small debt when God has so graciously dealt with you? (*Addresses on the First Epistle to the Corinthians, page 185*).

The different aspects of Christ's redemptive work are not given here in any chronological order; they all occurred simultaneously. The washing is related in other passages to that aspect of salvation which is known as regeneration; compare "the washing of regeneration"(Titus 3:5). The inclusion of sanctification in the list makes plain that this is not a reference to a "second work of grace" or any subsequent event. This is that aspect of sanctification which is known as positional. The believer has been set apart to God the moment he believes. Justification is that aspect of salvation which pertains to the believer's perfect standing before God, apart from all condemnation. He has been "declared righteous."

There is difference of opinion about verse 12. Some interpreters believe that another person interjected the words, "All things are lawful for me," to which Paul replied, "But all things are not helpful." If indeed Paul himself was making the whole statement, as seems more likely, then the "all things" must be taken in the context; that is, within the area of doubtful matters, things that are not specifically either commanded or prohibited. This is the beginning of Paul's dealing with how a Christian is to make decisions about doubtful matters. Behavior is to be based on principles found in the word of God, since scripture does not specifically legislate on every detail of behavior under all possible circumstances.

The relevant questions in discerning such principles are: How does this action affect myself? How does it affect my relationship to God? How does it affect my influence on other people?

In verse 12 Paul was considering the effect on himself. He rejected those practices that were not helpful or profitable (KJV, "expedient") as well as those that would enslave him. At any rate, the passage does not authorize anyone's taking sexual immorality as one of the so-called doubtful matters. It is singled out here as being different from other types of misconduct because of its effect on one's own body and personality.

The usual argument for taking immorality as of no consequence follows this fallacious reasoning: God has given us the natural appetites and therefore it is right to satisfy them. There is the appetite for food and the stomach to digest it; therefore, it is right and proper to fulfill that appetite. This has some validity in regard to the appetite for food, although even here there is danger of excess. Scripture warns against gluttony.

The sexual appetite, however, is different. There is no necessity of exercising it in order to live. Scripture is full of warnings and instructions about self-control. This passage, like a number of others, grounds sexual behavior in God's original creative purpose. Sex was indissolubly linked by God the creator with his ordinance of marriage. A sexual relationship between two persons, whether it is legitimate or illegitimate, links those two persons into what God calls "one flesh." Once such a union has occurred, it can never be denied as though it had never happened. The sin can be forgiven, but the consequences go on and on. David's sin illustrates this vividly (2 Samuel 12:10-14).

When a person becomes a believer, he is joined to the Lord Jesus Christ as "one spirit with Him" (6:17). Consequently, the believer must consider not only the effect of this conduct on himself, but also on the Lord. The repeated command in regard to sexual temptation is not to trifle with it, and certainly not to indulge it, but to run away from it. "Flee sexual immorality" (6:18; cf. 2 Timothy 2:22). Joseph is seen in scripture as an example of the kind of behavior befitting a godly person (Genesis 39:8,9,12).

The realization that one is joined to the Lord Jesus ought to be the strongest incentive to avoid an illicit sexual connection of any kind (6:15). The translation of me genoito as "God forbid" in KJV seems to get closer to the original in expressing the unmitigated horror of doing any such thing, even though it is not as literal as the modern versions: NKJV,"Certainly not!"; NASB, "May it never be!"; NIV, "Never!".

The thought that Paul expressed in chapter 3 concerning the church as a temple, or dwelling place of God, is now applied to the body of the individual believer. The permanent indwelling of the believer by the Holy Spirit is a distinctive New Testament doctrine and experience, based on the promise of the Lord Jesus in John 14:16. In the Old Testament the Holy Spirit sovereignly came upon individuals at particular times for particular purposes and withdrew according to his own purpose and will. Since the death, resurrection, and ascension of the Lord Jesus and the giving of the Holy Spirit at Pentecost, his presence in the believer is a permanent indwelling. The word for "temple" (naos) means a "sanctuary," the place where God and the worshiper meet.

In this case, the presence of the Holy Spirit indicates ownership. He is not there as a guest who will sometime depart, and certainly not as an interloper who will be asked to leave, but as the rightful possessor of the sanctuary. "Do you not know that . . . you are not your own?" The broad area of Christian stewardship is wrapped up in these few simple words.

The reason the Christian is not his own is that he has been purchased. The purchase price is not stated here, but is clearly defined in other passages as "his own blood" or "the precious blood of Christ" (Acts 20:28; 1 Peter 1:18-20). This aspect of Christ's saving work is comprehended under the doctrine of redemption (Ephesians 1:7; Colossians 1:14).

Man belongs to God by right of creation, but is in rebellion against his maker. Through the death of Christ, man has been placed into a new relationship, for a new and even more pressing claim has been put upon him. This relationship, as intimated previously, is expressed by the word *redeemed.* We have been bought with a price.

God, therefore, has a double claim on the Christian. But God does not want any unwilling, sullen slaves who have to serve him because they have no choice. It is as though he says to the believer in the Lord Jesus Christ, "Yes, you are mine because I made you; and doubly mine because I have redeemed you; but I want you to be mine because you want to be mine."

The critical text, as represented for example in the Aland-United Bible Societies reading, ends after the word *body* in verse 20. The attestation for the genuineness of the remainder of the verse is given in *The Greek New Testament According to the Majority Text.*

The incipient heresy of gnosticism was already beginning to creep into the church during Paul's ministry. It is seen as more fully developed a few years after this epistle in the false teachings encountered by the believers in Colosse.

In ethical conduct the gnostics followed two very divergent paths. Some of them said that the body, like all matter, was evil; therefore, it did not make any difference what they did with their bodies. Only the spirit counted for anything. Obviously these gnostics were libertines who abandoned all moral constraints.

In contrast, others were extreme ascetics. Since the body was evil, they said, only the life of the spirit was significant, and the body must be ignored or humiliated.

The gospel combats both of these extremes and everything in between in the teachings of the gnostics.

PART TWO

Things the Corinthians Had Written to Paul
1 Corinthians 7–16

SUBJECT ONE
Marriage, Separation, and Divorce
1 Corinthians 7

MARRIAGE (7:1–9)

7:1 Now concerning the things of which you wrote to me: It is good for a man not to touch a woman.

7:2 Nevertheless, because of sexual immorality, let each man have his own wife, and let each woman have her own husband.

7:3 Let the husband render to his wife the affection due her, and likewise also the wife to her husband.

7:4 The wife does not have authority over her own body, but the husband does. And likewise the husband does not have authority over his own body, but the wife does.

7:5 Do not deprive one another except with consent for a time, that you may give yourselves to fasting and prayer; and come together again so that Satan does not tempt you because of your lack of self-control.

7:6 But I say this as a concession, not as a commandment.

7:7 For I wish that all men were even as I myself. But each one has his own gift from God, one in this manner and another in that.

7:8 But I say to the unmarried and to the widows: It is good for them if they remain even as I am;

7:9 But if they cannot exercise self-control, let them marry. For it is better to marry than to burn with passion.

The phrase, "now concerning," marks the beginning of the second major division of the epistle, which includes various subjects about which the Corinthian church had requested Paul's instruction and counsel. The Greek phrase, *peri de*, used to mark off the different topics, occurs in 7:1; 7:25; 8:1; 12:1; 16:1; and 16:12.

This passage introduces one of the most controversial subjects in scripture. Sex, which was given by God as a great blessing for mankind, has been perverted, misused, and abused through sin.

In the study of any topic or doctrine in scripture one must follow an inductive method, searching out facts here and there and drawing general conclusions from many particulars. Some have made the mistake seemingly of taking this chapter as the sum total of what Paul taught about marriage. This is only a part of a wide area that includes the basis of God's ordinance of marriage from the time of creation. The sexual aspect, which is discussed in the present text, is obviously of great importance—absolutely vital to the subject of marriage—and must not be neglected. Neither, however, should it be understood as exhausting the subject.

Even in the first and second generations of the church's history asceticism was beginning to manifest itself. This developed later into monasticism, the "celibacy of the clergy," and the attempt to portray the single life as more holy than the married state. At the other extreme was the idea of some that everyone must marry, as though the single person were an incomplete individual and unable to live a holy life.

Paul's opening statement does not overly exalt either celibacy or matrimony. He asserted that it is possible for a single person, whether man or woman, to live a chaste life within the will of God. Note that scripture does not use the word *better*, but the word *good*. The celibate life can be a good life if it is within the will of God for an individual. "Not to touch a woman" is a euphemism for sexual relations. Sex as given by God is to be experienced within marriage, not before it or outside of it, and it is obviously for one *man* and one *woman*. This rules out premarital and extramarital sex, polygamy and polyandry, and, of course, homosexual marriage. Note God's severe judgment on abuses of sex in Leviticus 18 and 20, with the imposition of the death penalty in the theocracy of Israel for various kinds of sexual sins.

As indicated above, some interpreters speak of Paul's "low estimate" of marriage, alleging that he viewed it only as a lesser evil than sexual immorality. The Holy Spirit, knowing the tendencies of humanity to misuse even the best gifts of God, graciously reminds us that God has provided the wonderful and beautiful institution of marriage, and within marriage the gift of sexuality, furnishing a legitimate and satisfying release for that natural and legitimate drive. This is the fulfillment of God's design in creation. "The two shall become one flesh" (Matthew 19:5; cf. Genesis 2:24). In the Genesis account we are informed of the unashamed nakedness of the primeval pair, a further indication of the holiness of God-ordained marriage (cf. Genesis 2:25 and Hebrews 13:4).

Another passage closely related to this, but viewing marriage from a different perspective, is in Ephesians 5, especially verse 32: "This is a great mystery, but I speak concerning Christ and the church." Although that added teaching of the spiritual significance of marriage is not found in the present passage, the two ideas are not incompatible; in fact, they form a magnificent whole. God has purposely created this most intimate and beautiful of all human relationships to be a symbol of that even more wonderful relationship of Christ and the church. In the Old Testament there are a number of bridegroom-bride types setting forth this spiritual relationship: Adam and Eve, Isaac and Rebekah, Joseph and Asenath, Boaz and Ruth, Solomon and Shulamith. The glorious fulfillment is found in the closing section of the book of Revelation (21:2,9).

One must not suppose, however, that verse 2 states a command for all people to marry. The context shows that Paul recognized that some will not marry, for various reasons. Verse 2 stresses the God-intended and God-appointed monogamy as distinguished from bigamous and polygamous unions, which apparently originated with Lamech in the line of Cain (Genesis 4:19) and toward which even many of the people of Israel, including famous rulers such as David and Solomon, drifted away from God's ideal appointment.

A promiscuous society, like that of Corinth and that of our own day, demonstrates by contrast the divine wisdom of God's marriage appointment. This is in harmony with instructions in the Old Testament (note especially Proverbs 5:15-20).

There is some slight textual variation in verse 3 and difference of opinion as to whether there is reference to the so-called conjugal duty or whether the apostle is speaking of a manifestation of affection. Ascetic interpreters have sometimes mistakenly thought that the sexual aspect of marriage is something only tolerated by God, not of his appointment.

Verse 4 spells out plainly the mutuality in this most intimate of human relationships. This seems to be a missing ingredient in the sexually haphazard culture around us today.

G.C. Luck expressed this thought well. "In true marriage there are not only joys but also responsibilities. When a person chooses to enter such a condition, then he or she should be prepared to assume these responsibilities. Mentioned first with regard to such obligations is a matter not of action but of *attitude*. Wife and husband are to render to each other *due benevolence*."

The notion of ascetics—that married people ought to live as though they were unmarried (thus somehow presuming to be purer and holier)—is contrary to scripture and is, in fact, a flagrant disobedience to this text. The real author of this false philosophy is named in verse 5. The married person who does not find sexual satisfaction with his or her spouse, as God intended, will be much more likely to sin in this vital area. The deeply satisfying climax and release in which the sexual aspect of marriage reflects the total spiritual, intellectual, emotional, and physical union appointed and approved by God emphasizes our heavenly Father's gracious provisions for mankind. God's instruction to the married partners is that they are not to deprive one another, certainly not on a unilateral basis. By mutual agreement they may refrain from the normal sexual relationship, but only for a limited time to be devoted to spiritual purposes ("fasting and prayer"). Prolonged abstinence may lead to marital problems.

Too many Christians seem to think that sex was created by the devil—an obvious lie. Certainly the devil has done and will do what he can to twist and pervert God's handiwork. Selfish exploitation of one's spouse for one's own pleasure, without regard for the spouse's welfare, is a perversion of what God intended. In this, as in other areas of life, true giving of self in love approaches the realization of the heavenly Father's ideal. The Song of Songs celebrates true marriage as it pictures the bridegroom and the bride in loving, happy contemplation of each other, each discovering the deepest pleasure in giving pleasure to the other.

It is a sad and ironic misreading of history to blame the Puritan ethic as the cause of unhappiness and gloom in marriage. No doubt many Puritans were culpable, but it has been the libertines who have mistaken hedonism for real and lasting pleasure, and thus have perverted the holy purpose that God put into marriage. One such libertine, the poet George Gordon, Lord Byron, wrote out of bitter reaction, "The worm, the canker and the grief are mine alone" ("On My Thirty-sixth Year").

God's children have the capability of building a marriage that will glorify him and contain a lifelong satisfaction, in which the sexual aspect of marriage, exercised according to God's plan, will enhance and enrich the complete relationship.

Verse 6 refers to the principle in verse 2, not to the intervening verses; that is, even though God's will is for most people to marry, there are exceptions, such as Paul himself (whose situation is referred to again in 9:5). In verse 7 Paul recognized that God's will is not the same for all in this matter: "Each one has his own gift from God."

Note the word *good* again in verse 8 (cf. 7:1). Again he did not use the word *better.* Recognizing, however, that not everyone has the capability of "self-control" required for living a chaste life as a single person, again the apostle advised marriage. "For it is better to marry than to burn with passion." Viewed in the context of the biblical teaching on marriage as a whole, this is not a choice of the "lesser evil," but simply using to advantage that state in which one finds oneself. As one commentator has said, the text says that while it is better to marry than to burn, it also certainly implies that it is better to burn than to sin (i.e., commit sins of immorality).

COMMANDS TO THE MARRIED (7:10-16)

7:10 Now to the married I command, yet not I but the Lord: A wife is not to depart from her husband.

7:11 But even if she does depart, let her remain unmarried or be reconciled to her husband. And a husband is not to divorce his wife.

7:12 But to the rest I, not the Lord, say: If any brother has a wife who does not believe, and she is willing to live with him, let him not divorce her.

7:13 And a woman who has a husband who does not believe, if he is willing to live with her, let her not divorce him.

7:14 For the unbelieving husband is sanctified by the wife,

and the unbelieving wife is sanctified by the husband; otherwise your children would be unclean, but
now they are holy.

7:15 But if the unbeliever departs, let him depart; a
brother or a sister is not under bondage in such
cases. But God has called us to peace.

7:16 For how do you know, O wife, whether you will save
your husband? Or how do you know, O husband,
whether you will save your wife?

Paul now moved from instructions concerning getting married
to commands to those already married. As an apostle he had a
right to speak authoritatively, but he did not need to give any new
instruction in the first instance because the Lord Jesus Christ
spoke directly to this point during his earthly ministry (see
Matthew 5:31-32; 19:1-12; Mark 10:1-12; Luke 16:18).

There are many divisions among interpreters concerning marriage and divorce for Christians. Some, on the basis of the Mark
and Luke passages, insist that divorce is always wrong and contrary to the will of God, and that remarriage is never permissible
for a divorced person. The exception mentioned by the Lord in
the Matthew passage is then taken to refer to unfaithfulness during the Jewish betrothal period and hence not applicable today
(see *Ryrie Study Bible* notes on Matthew 5:32 and 19:10).

The term *porneia*, used by the Lord Jesus as the permitted
ground for divorce, is the word for sexual immorality in general.
It would seem to be best to interpret the parallel passages as a
unit. Mark and Luke state the general principle, for there is no
doubt that God hates divorce; he says so in so many words
(Malachi 2:16). There are, however, some circumstances that
make divorce permissible. On the basis of the passages in
Matthew many Christians believe that the Lord Jesus distin-
guishes between the innocent partner and the offending partner,
and that sexual unfaithfulness on the part of one makes divorce
permissible for the other, even though not mandatory in every
case, for there is the recognition that the offender may become
truly repentant and may seek forgiveness, reconciliation, and
restoration.

Paul stated that the Lord Jesus gave the general principle, and
we believe he gave one ground of exception to the rule. This bars
the third major area of interpretation, which is widely held and

practiced by unbelievers and unfortunately has become more and more usual in the church: easy divorce for almost any cause. This is certainly not the teaching of the Bible, although it seems to have been the practice of many of the people of Israel in Old Testament times.

Paul's statement, then, is fully in harmony with the words of the Lord Jesus ("yet not I, but the Lord").

Further complication comes in verse 12. This has been wrongfully interpreted and applied by those who say that this was only Paul's opinion and that he disclaimed the Lord's authority for making this statement. The sense of the passage is very different. What Paul said is that on the subject he was now to consider, the Lord Jesus did not even speak during his earthly ministry. Therefore, it was necessary for Paul, as a duly appointed apostle and representative of the Lord, to give an official pronouncement. There are at least two reasons why this area was treated in this way.

First, there is the Old Testament experience, and what Paul was saying is very different from that. The people of Israel were forbidden by God to intermarry with those of surrounding nations, who were for the most part idolaters. In the days of Ezra and Nehemiah many men of the returned remnant of Israel had taken foreign wives. This was a great grief to Ezra, Nehemiah, and other godly people in Israel. Consequently such men were commanded to put away these wives (obviously making material provision for them and for their children). This is the burden of Nehemiah 13.

The second reason which made it urgent for Paul to speak as an inspired apostle was that the Lord Jesus had not spoken directly to this kind of situation. In fact, such a situation could not have developed until after our Lord's death and resurrection and the subsequent preaching of the gospel. Apparently, some of the Corinthian Christians were regarding the Old Testament history and practice as the norm for their behavior. Their line of reasoning seems to have been that just as the believing Jews had to put away their foreign wives, so a Christian should divorce his or her unbelieving spouse.

The situations, however, were very different. There is no such ethnic mandate in the church as there was on the nation of Israel in the Old Testament. It is clear that the commands given here are for cases in which one of the married partners has become a Christian after marrying. Scripture plainly forbids marriage of a believer with an unbeliever (7:39; cf. 2 Corinthians 6:14-18). But as the gospel spread and people responded in faith, inevitably there would be families in which one spouse believed in the Lord Jesus and the other did not. The Corinthian believers were sincerely perplexed about what to do. Furthermore, the Lord Jesus had not spoken to this. He could not, because the precise conditions had not arisen when he was here on earth.

Paul, therefore, authoritatively taught and commanded that the believing partner is not to seek separation or divorce. In the face of this terminology it is hardly tenable to say, as some do, that this section does not deal with divorce (cf. G. Archer, *Encyclopedia of Bible Difficulties*).

Verse 14 is a controversial one. The word *sanctified* must not be equated with the word *saved*, for nobody can be saved through another's faith, only by his own. The root meaning of "sanctify" is to set apart. The teaching seems to be that the unbelieving partner is placed in a relationship which may be used to his eternal advantage, in that he hears the gospel and sees it lived out in his spouse's daily conduct. He has someone to pray for his salvation and to be his intercessor before the Lord. This will be also to the benefit of the children, who will have opportunity for a Christian upbringing, which would be totally lacking if both parents were unbelievers. Although they will feel the influences of the unbelieving world, they will also experience the blessing and joy of their believing parent's relationship to the Lord Jesus Christ.

The believing spouse cannot prevent the unbelieving one from leaving. The difference of opinion among interpreters pertains chiefly to the word *bondage* in verse 15. Does it mean merely that the believer is not bound to try to stop the unbelieving partner, but simply to let him go and remain legally married to him without any thought of divorce and remarriage? This is widely held, but it does not seem to do justice to the word *bondage*. It seems more likely that the Holy Spirit is classifying this type of desertion as a breaking of the marriage vows (as also in the case of adultery), which leaves the believing partner free to remarry. Again we should emphasize that the Christian spouse is not required to remarry. He or she may choose to remain unmarried. In that case the instructions of verses 39 and 40 are appropriate, although given for a different situation.

People can propound an almost infinite number of vexing variations of this theme. Scripture does not cover every conceivable divergence from the general subject, but furnishes us with principles that are to be applied in our own experience—not to be ignored or stretched out of shape to enable one to have his own way with scripture rather than obeying scripture teachings.

In other words, the Christian should not be constantly looking for loopholes to get himself out of an unpleasant condition, but should be asking himself, "What does God say about this, and how does he want me to act on it?" The person who has been married, divorced,remarried, and then saved cannot undo the past. He must allow the Lord to confront him where he is and to go on from there, obeying the principles of scripture from the point where scripture took him in.

It is heartening to know that sometimes God uses the testimony of the believing partner in a mixed marriage of this type to lead the unbelieving partner to saving faith in Jesus Christ. Peter especially showed how this applies to a Christian wife married to a non-Christian husband (1 Peter 3:1-2).

REMAINING IN THE ORIGINAL CALLING (7:17-24)

7:17 But as God has distributed to each one, as the Lord has called each one, so let him walk. And so I ordain in all the churches.

7:18 Was anyone called while circumcised? Let him not become uncircumcised. Was anyone called while uncircumcised? Let him not be circumcised.

7:19 Circumcision is nothing and uncircumcision is nothing, but keeping the commandments of God is what matters.

7:20 Let each one remain in the same calling in which he was called.

7:21 Were you called while a slave? Do not be concerned about it; but if you can be made free, rather use it.

7:22 For he who is called in the Lord while a slave is the Lord's freedman. Likewise he who is called while free is Christ's slave.

> 7:23 You were bought at a price; do not become slaves of men.
>
> 7:24 Brethren, let each one remain with God in that state in which he was called.

The teaching of remaining in the original calling is applied here more broadly than just to marriage. It should be remembered that scripture is enunciating general principles. Paul himself was an outstanding example of the truth of 7:18a, while Titus was a perfect example of the truth of 7:18b. Paul would not surrender the right of Christian liberty to the Judaizers, who were insisting that gentiles must become Jews in order to be saved (Galatians 2:3-5).

Yet some have accused Paul of inconsistency because he arranged for Timothy to be circumcised (Acts 16:1-3). The background in Acts 16:1 emphasizes that Timothy was half Jewish. Paul saw no conflict here in simply becoming "all things to all men" (1 Corinthians 9:22), in not unnecessarily giving offense. Since Timothy was not a gentile, the principle of gentile liberty was not at stake here.

As in many other places in scripture, the emphasis is put on the inner being: the heart. Outward circumstances are inconsequential in comparison to one's personal relationship to God through the Lord Jesus Christ (cf. Romans 2:25-29).

"Keeping the commandments of God is what matters" (7:19). The last three words have been supplied aptly by the translators; this is clearly the implied thought of the original. Relationship to Christ transcends all other relationships; therefore, one ought not to make one's earthly condition, which is temporary and in some cases superficial, more important than it really is. That the principle of remaining, or abiding, is not absolute is shown by the wording of 7:21. The slave does not have to remain a slave if he has a legitimate opportunity to be free, but he should not waste his time and energy wishing to be free; instead, he should use his influence for Christ (even though it be small) in either condition. Earthly rank will not last forever. The most oppressed slave, on becoming a Christian has entered into the glorious liberty of the sons of God, while the free man in the eyes of the law has the privilege and responsibility of being like Paul in the company of that greatest and most gracious of masters, the Lord himself.

The word *slave* is often translated in our English versions as "servant," but that word does not bring out the full meaning in a passage such as this.

"You are bought at a price" (7:23). This is the second time Paul reminded his readers of the cost of their redemption (cf. 6:19). Even a free person in the eyes of the law could make himself a slave of men by mistakenly subjecting himself out of fear, misunderstanding, cowardice, or false zeal to the thoughts and foibles of men. The clear teaching of this passage is that the individual's relationship to God through the Lord Jesus Christ is to be the standard or norm for his entire behavior, rising above earthly, material, and temporal relationships and responsibilities.

SPECIAL INSTRUCTIONS CONCERNING VIRGINS (7:25-40)

7:25 Now concerning virgins: I have no commandment from the Lord; yet I give judgment as one whom the Lord in His mercy has made trustworthy.

7:26 I suppose therefore that this is good because of the present distress—that it is good for a man to remain as he is:

7:27 Are you bound to a wife? Do not seek to be loosed. Are you loosed from a wife? Do not seek a wife.

7:28 But even if you do marry, you have not sinned; and if a virgin marries, she has not sinned. Nevertheless such will have trouble in the flesh, but I would spare you.

7:29 But this I say, brethren, the time is short, so that from now on even those who have wives should be as though they had none,

7:30 those who weep as though they did not weep, those who rejoice as though they did not rejoice, those who buy as though they did not possess,

7:31 and those who use this world as not misusing it. For the form of this world is passing away.

7:32 But I want you to be without care. He who is unmarried cares for the things of the Lord—how he may please the Lord.

7:33 But he who is married cares about the things of the world—how he may please his wife.

7:34 There is a difference between a wife and a virgin. The unmarried woman cares about the things of the Lord, that she may be holy both in body and in spirit. But she who is married about the things of the world—how she may please her husband.

7:35 And this I say for your own profit, not that I may put a leash on you, but for what is proper, and that you may serve the Lord without distraction.

7:36 But if any man thinks he is behaving improperly toward his virgin, if she is past the flower of youth, and thus it must be, let him do what he wishes. He does not sin; let them marry.

7:37 Nevertheless he who stands steadfast in his heart, having no necessity, but has power over his own will, and has so determined in his heart that he will keep his virgin, does well.

7:38 So then he who gives her in marriage does well, but he who does not give her in marriage does better.

7:39 A wife is bound by law as long as her husband lives; but if her husband dies, she is at liberty to be married to whom she wishes, only in the Lord.

7:40 But she is happier if she remains as she is, according to my judgment—and I think I also have the Spirit of God.

As in the case of many crucial passages of scripture, it is far easier to say what this section does not mean than to say what it means. The two major forms of interpretation are: first, that the instructions are given to a man seeking a wife; and second, that they are given to the father or other close male relative who has the responsibility for arranging a proper marriage for his daughter or close female relative.

At the outset, however, the phrase "because of the present distress" (verse 26) seems to mark this portion as being affected by particular and perhaps temporary conditions which the Corinthians were facing. It has often been said that these believers were approaching severe persecution and that the apostle's injunctions here concerning marriage are to be understood in that light. All through the church's history there have been conditions like these in some parts of the world to which these words would be especially applicable. Obviously the passage cannot be taken to refer to permanent situations in which the church finds itself, in the light of what Paul had already written about every man having his own wife and every woman having her own husband (7:2). Furthermore, the use of "now concerning" (*peri de*) at the beginning of verse 25 marks this off as a distinct topic from that just discussed in 7:1-24.

There is a general principle here that must be considered. There are situations, conditions, or places in the Lord's service in which marriage may be inadvisable, even though not forbidden. The words of the Lord Jesus in Matthew 19:11-12 are applicable in this connection.

The apostle was not expressing either horror or indifference about the usual actions and intentions of married people, but simply stating a fact of life that the married man has taken on responsibilities toward his wife and family that sometimes limit his sphere of service for the Lord. This would be intensified in a time of persecution, such as Paul evidently had in mind in this passage.

We should note also that again we are facing a generalization, even though an inspired one. The text does not say or mean that every unmarried person is more attentive to doing the Lord's will than every married person is. We so often want a complete and final answer to every individual situation, hoping for some ready-made solution that follows automatically. God's guidance is never mechanical. He always leads as his Spirit applies the word of God to the believing and surrendered heart. This avoids a false mysticism, which may identify every passing thought and whim as the mind of the Spirit, but also avoids a mechanical idea of guidance, which supposes that scripture directly addresses every conceivable condition. In the case of either of these extremes, there is a sacrifice of human freedom within the God-appointed sphere of his guidance. The believer must continually search the scriptures, continually pray, and continually be willing and ready to obey the clearly stated principles of scripture.

Authorities differ on the meaning of verses 36-40, whether these instructions are for prospective bridegrooms or for fathers who must arrange suitable marriages for their virgin daughters. Translation committees are often divided, with the result that whichever view is given in the text often has an alternative in the margin. The four most widely used standard evangelical translations exhibit this pattern:

1 CORINTHIANS 7:36

Version	Text	Margin
KJV	"his virgin"	
NKJV	"his virgin"	"his virgin daughter"
NIV	"the virgin he is engaged to"	"his daughter"
NASB	"his virgin daughter"	

The preponderance among versions extensively used by evangelical Christians seems to be for the idea of addressing the prospective husband. There is a serious difficulty, however, with the Greek verb *gamizo* in verse 38. Is it synonymous with *gameo*, which means "to marry"? *Gamizo* normally means "to give in marriage" or "to cause to be married." Grammatically the meaning would seem to be "to give in marriage." It must be confessed that this interpretation seems awkward in the text, but perhaps some of this is caused by our unfamiliarity with the marriage customs of that day. In this case NASB seems to be the most literal and grammatical of the commonly used versions among evangelicals. It should be noted that Arndt and Gingrich lean toward the idea of taking *gamizo* as synonymous with *gameo*.

Needless to say, a corruption of the passage arose very early in the ascetic idea of "spiritual marriage," in which a man and a woman, taking what came to be called "holy orders," lived in the same house together but refrained from the sexual aspects of marriage, a mistaken idea of the marriage relationship, which often led to sexual sin.

Again, in the instructions about widows in verses 39 and 40, we see principles to be followed. Christian liberty does not include freedom for a Christian to marry an unsaved person. That part is perfectly clear. But there is no obligation to remarry. In fact, Paul gave it as a general principle that in many instances widows would be better off to remain unmarried. That this is not a direct and universal command, however, is seen by comparison with 1 Timothy 5:14, where Paul counseled younger widows to remarry.

SUBJECT TWO
Christian Liberty
1 Corinthians 8–10

MEAT OFFERED TO IDOLS (8:1-13)

8:1 Now concerning things offered to idols: We know that we all have knowledge. Knowledge puffs up, but love edifies.

8:2 And if anyone thinks that he knows anything, he knows nothing yet as he ought to know.

8:3 But if anyone loves God, this one is known by Him.

8:4 Therefore concerning the eating of things offered to idols, we know that an idol is nothing in the world, and that there is no other God but one.

8:5 For even if there are so-called gods, whether in heaven or on earth (as there are many gods and many lords),

8:6 yet for us there is one God, the Father, of whom are all things, and we for Him; and one Lord Jesus Christ, through whom are all things, and through whom we live.

8:7 However, there is not in everyone that knowledge; for some, with consciousness of the idol, until now eat it as a thing offered to an idol; and their conscience, being weak, is defiled.

8:8 But food does not commend us to God; for neither if we eat are we the better, nor if we do not eat are we the worse.

8:9 But beware lest somehow this liberty of yours become a stumbling block to those who are weak.

8:10 For if anyone sees you who have knowledge eating in an idol's temple, will not the conscience of him who is weak be emboldened to eat those things offered to idols?

8:11 And because of your knowledge shall the weak brother perish, for whom Christ died?

8:12 But when you thus sin against the brethren, and wound their weak conscience, you sin against Christ.

8:13 Therefore, if food makes my brother stumble, I will never again eat meat, lest I make my brother stumble.

The particular problem which lies at the heart of this section is that of meat offered to idols, a very direct dilemma with the Corinthian Christians, even though it seems alien to us today. This particular difficulty, however, serves to illustrate a number of truths concerning the entire question of Christian liberty.

Paul introduced his treatment of the question in chapter 8 and drew the whole matter to a conclusion in chapter 10, using the intervening chapter 9 to apply some of these principles to his own experience. It should be noted that he approached the question of meat offered to idols from three lines. First, how does this affect my own Christian life? Does it help or hinder? Second, what effect does it have on others? Does it encourage spiritual growth or decline? Finally, what effect does it have on my relationship to God? Is it useful to me? Is it helpful to others? Is it for the glory of God?

Many of the ancient religions involved animal sacrifice, no doubt a corrupt application of the primeval instructions God gave after Adam and Eve sinned in the garden of Eden. "By faith Abel offered to God a more excellent sacrifice than Cain" (Hebrews 11:4). Since Abel offered "by faith," God must have given a previous command about sacrifice to which Abel responded positively and Cain reacted negatively. Oral tradition concerning animal sacrifice obviously was carried to all parts of the world as the descendants of Noah spread abroad after the flood.

The problem of the Corinthians was threefold. First, was it right or permissible to attend a feast in a pagan idol temple? Second, was it right to buy in the public market meat that was known to have been offered to idols? Finally, what about accepting a dinner invitation to the home of unbelievers where it was reasonably certain that the meat had been offered to idols?

Briefly, the answer Paul gave to the first question is no; to the second, yes; and to the third, yes and no, or maybe. We shall examine this more carefully as we go through the text.

At the beginning of his treatment of this rather complex problem the apostle, agreeing that we all have knowledge—implying that this knowledge pertains to the foolishness of idolatry and the non-existence of idols—nevertheless insisted that the foundational principle on which answers are to be given is not knowledge, but love. While knowledge tends to "puff up," love "builds up" ("edifies"). The person who supposes he has superior knowledge and who is intending to settle the question merely on the basis of that knowledge, is self-deceived: "He knows nothing yet as he ought to know" (8:2).

The contrast is to love God. One who truly loves him will want to do what he wants. When the issue is presented in this way it is not an academic or theoretical question in which opponents debate and judges decide who is more effective in presenting his arguments, but all concerned are seeking what is best for all.

The intellectual aspect of the problem is quite clear. We believers know that any idol is a "nothing," a nonentity (8:4). Consequently anything offered to an idol has not really been offered to a "god" at all. There is only one God, the living and true God, the God and Father of our Lord Jesus Christ. This is definitely established in verses 4 through 6.

"However . . ." (8:7). There is another aspect to the problem, which removes it from the merely intellectual realm. *People* are to be considered. Not everyone has this knowledge that an idol is not real. Such people would be terribly bothered to think they are eating food that has been (supposedly) blessed by a "god" to whom it has been offered. To sit down to a feast in an idol temple would seem to be an endorsement of that god and that worship, or at least an acknowledgment of his (her, or its) reality and authority. Such a person's conscience would be "defiled," Paul stated. Conscience, while imperfect and marred by sin, is God-given and ought not to be disregarded.

You may eat and not be harmed, because you know that the whole paraphernalia of temple, idol, sacrifice, feast, etc. have no validity. While you are enjoying yourself and boasting about your Christian liberty, a less knowledgeable Christian, following your example, has found this a real stumbling block and has been set back in his Christian experience and growth.

It should be understood that this passage is not dealing with questions and problems clearly answered in scripture or with behavior that is definitely forbidden. This is one of the "doubtful" matters, also discussed in Romans 14.

Put in the entire context, however, the answer must be in the negative. Once the believer has admitted that his example may lead some other believer astray, he has voluntarily given up his individual freedom. It then becomes wrong for him. Paul put it in strong terms, accusing such believers of sinning "against Christ" (8:12) and vowing that in such circumstances he would give up his freedom and "never again eat meat."

Should Christians participate in a feast in an idol temple? Certainly not. There is further elucidation of this in chapter 10.

PAUL'S PERSONAL LIMITATION OF HIS LIBERTY (9:1-18)

9:1 Am I not an apostle? Am I not free? Have I not seen Jesus Christ our Lord? Are you not my work in the Lord?

9:2 If I am not an apostle to others, yet doubtless I am to you. For you are the seal of my apostleship in the Lord.

9:3 My defense to those who examine me is this:

9:4 Do we have no right to eat and drink?

9:5 Do we have no right to take along a believing wife, as do also the other apostles, the brothers of the Lord, and Cephas?

9:6 Or is it only Barnabas and I who have no right to refrain from working?

9:7 Who ever goes to war at his own expense? Who plants a vineyard and does not eat of its fruit? Or who tends a flock and does not drink of the milk of the flock?

9:8 Do I say these things as a mere man? Or does not the law say the same also?

9:9 For it is written in the law of Moses, "You shall not muzzle an ox while it treads out the grain." Is it oxen God is concerned about?

9:10 Or does He say it altogether for our sakes? For our sakes, no doubt, this is written, that he who plows should plow in hope, and he who threshes in hope should be partaker of his hope.

9:11 If we have sown spiritual things for you, is it a great thing if we reap your material things?

9:12 If others are partakers of this right over you, are we not even more? Nevertheless we have not used this right, but endure all things lest we hinder the gospel of Christ.

9:13 Do you not know that those who minister the holy things eat of the things of the temple, and those who serve at the altar partake of the offerings of the altar?

9:14 Even so the Lord has commanded that those who preach the gospel should live from the gospel.

9:15 But I have used none of these things, nor have I written these things that it should be done so to me; for it would be better for me to die than that anyone should make my boasting void.

9:16 For if I preach the gospel, I have nothing to boast of, for necessity is laid upon me; yes, woe is me if I do not preach the gospel!

9:17 For if I do this willingly, I have a reward; but if against my will, I have been entrusted with a stewardship.

9:18 What is my reward then? That when I preach the gospel, I may present the gospel of Christ without charge, that I may not abuse my authority in the gospel.

The rhetorical questions with which Paul opened this section show a personal application of the principles introduced in chapter 8. The grammatical form of the questions required the answer yes. He moved from his own identity and condition to the fact that they themselves were his "work in the Lord" (9:1) and reinforced it with the reminder that they had come to Christ through his ministry (cf. 4:15 above). For this reason they were the "seal" of his apostleship; that is, their very existence as saved persons came through his proclamation of the gospel, and this attested to the fact that he was truly an apostle, a special emissary of Christ to them.

The apostle used Barnabas and himself as examples of the right exercise of Christian liberty. Again, each of the series of questions requires the answer yes. "Right to eat and drink" means, of course, the right to eat and drink at the expense of the churches. In the next question Paul asserted his right to claim support for his wife also, if he had a wife. This is purely hypothetical because the Corinthians knew that Paul was not married.

Certainly Paul was unmarried at the time he wrote this epistle (7:7). There is scarcely any disagreement about that; the difference comes in the question whether he was a widower or a bachelor. Those who believe he was a widower base their belief on his supposed membership in the Sanhedrin, the Jewish supreme council. One of the possible qualifications for membership was that the member be a married man.

The only tangible evidence for Paul's membership is his statement in Acts 26:10 in which he told Agrippa that he had "cast his vote"against Christians. It is doubtful that the verb used here was restricted to formal voting; it may simply indicate Paul's rabid support of what the council decided, for he was definitely an agent of the Sanhedrin, whether a member or not.

Some authorities assert that there is no proof anyway that marriage was required for membership in the Sanhedrin at that time. The language in which Paul described his state seems to fit bachelorhood better than widowerhood. There is no direct evidence that he ever was married. The argument from silence is often a shaky one, but it seems strange that there would be no hint of a marriage in the passages dealing with that important subject.

Verse 6 tells us little about Barnabas's situation. Apparently he had not brought a wife with him on his travels. Those who were accompanied by their wives included "the other apostles." This is taken by some to mean that Barnabas was officially an apostle, but it seems more likely that the word is being used here in its broader meaning.

An interesting dilemma confronts the Roman Catholic Church in insisting on the primacy of Peter as the first "pope" along with the dogma from ancient times on the "celibacy of the clergy." One of those healed by the Lord Jesus during His early Galilean ministry was Simon Peter's mother-in-law (Matthew 8:14-15). *Cephas* is the Aramaic equivalent of the Greek name *Peter*.

"The brothers of the Lord" were his half brothers, mentioned in Matthew 13:55, not his stepbrothers or his cousins as many allege in order to retain the unscriptural doctrine of the "perpet-

ual virginity of Mary." James is described by Paul in Galatians
1:19 as "the Lord's brother." He was prominent in the church at
Jerusalem and summed up the decision of the notable council
held there (Acts15:13-21).

To strengthen the force of his questions Paul appealed to
examples in everyday life. The soldier, the vinedresser, and the
dairyman are common, well-known illustrations of those who
receive support from their occupation.

In addition to the appeal to ordinary experience, Paul also
referred to the law. The passage, at first glance, would seem to
deny God's interest in oxen. This is, no doubt, hyperbolic language. Yes, there is a sense in which God cares for oxen, but that
is far less important than his care for his servants. The word *altogether* in verse 10 must be understood in its context (see Arndt
and Gingrich). NIV is helpful here; it translates *pantos* as "surely,"
which is sanctioned by Arndt and Gingrich.

It is only logical and right that those who had profited from the
apostle's spiritual ministry should contribute to his physical and
material welfare. They apparently had acknowledged this in
respect to other teachers and helpers. Why were they so reluc-
tant to apply the same principle to their actual spiritual father?

"Nevertheless we have not used this right"! Having gone to
some lengths to establish his right to expect support, he now
deliberately and conclusively rejected it. It appears that some
of the Corinthians were falsely accusing Paul of taking money
from them for his personal gain. For this reason he insisted on
supporting himself. Acts 18, which tells of Paul's first visit to
Corinth, brings out the fact that he pursued his trade of a tent
maker, along with Aquila and Priscilla during his sojourn in that
city.

But Paul had not finished with this subject. He returned to the
Old Testament scriptures and cited the example of the priests in
the sanctuary. "Even so . . ." Those who preach the gospel are
appointed by God to obtain their living from the gospel. There
is nothing wrong about a pastor's accepting a salary from a
church. Paul often accepted such money from other churches. In
fact he said that he "robbed other churches"; i.e., took dispro-
portionately from them in order not to be obligated to the
Corinthians, some of whom had evidently made an unnecessary
issue about these financial matters. Again he emphasized, "But

I have used none of these things," and showed how vital this subject was to him by preferring to die rather than give up his ground of boasting.

What was he boasting about? Was it the fact that he was preaching the gospel? No, not at all, for that was a necessity laid on him by the Lord Jesus himself at his conversion crisis (Acts 9:15-16). He might have lost any semblance of reward if he had done this grudgingly or halfheartedly, but that did not cancel his obligation to the Lord. The only ground of boasting in this connection was that he was able and willing to bring the gospel to them "without charge" (9:18).

The unreasonableness of some of the Corinthian believers is seen in that on one hand they criticized Paul for taking money for preaching the gospel, but when they discovered that he refused to take money from them and insisted on supporting himself by his trade, they criticized him just as severely, questioning his apostleship and authority, and saying that if he really were an apostle, he would claim support from them and give up his "secular" work. It was a no-win situation for the apostle.

"ALL THINGS TO ALL" (9:19-23)

9:19 For though I am free from all men, I have made myself a servant to all, that I might win the more;

9:20 and to the Jews I became as a Jew, that I might win Jews; to those who are under the law, as under the law, that I might win those who are under the law;

9:21 to those who are without law, as without law (not being without law toward God, but under law toward Christ), that I might win those who are without law;

9:22 to the weak I became as weak, that I might win the weak. I have become all things to all men, that I might by all means save some.

9:23 Now this I do for the gospel's sake, that I may be partaker of it with you.

This paragraph has been widely misunderstood and misapplied, as though Paul were endorsing partaking of other men's sins in order to make a good impression on them (but see Ephesians 5:7; 1 Timothy 5:22). Instead of this Paul was saying that he had tried to work with people on their own level and to give as little offense as possible in order to procure a hearing for the gospel. If he had shown utter disregard for the opinions and customs of others, they would have been less likely to listen to his preaching. To put this in the simplest terms, it is as though Paul were admonishing that if you want to give a testimony for Christ to an orthodox Jew, you don't begin by serving him ham for dinner.

"To the Jews I became as a Jew." But was not Paul a Jew? Yes, by birth and upbringing he was. In the sight of God, however, he was neither a Jew nor a gentile, but a member of the body of Christ (cf. 1 Corinthians 10:32). His actions in Jerusalem on his last visit there were in harmony with this principle. Some Bible interpreters express strong disagreement with what Paul did on this visit, and horror that the apostle of Christian liberty would take part in any of the rituals of Judaism. It seems most unlikely that he was denying anything he had previously written or spoken on the subject. He did not appear to have been aware of any inconsistency. It would be well to be very slow to criticize an apostle except in those instances in which scripture itself indicates wrongdoing, as it sometimes does (note, for example, Galatians 2:11). We can all profit from the Holy Spirit's warning against premature judgments on insufficient grounds (1 Corinthians 4:5).

In explaining his attitude toward those who were without the mosaic law, Paul was very careful to demonstrate that he was not lawless. Nevertheless he used language that would have had some meaning to his hearers. A good example of this is his address on the Areopagus in Athens (Acts 17), which is often criticized unjustly by many Bible students.

The Lord Jesus Christ himself followed this principle, so much so, in fact, that his enemies called him a "winebibber and a glutton," (Matthew 11:19; Luke 7:34) because he ate with tax collectors and sinners, two groups of especially despised people among the Jews of that day. Consideration for others lies at the root of this principle: recognition of the personhood of the individual without condoning wrongdoing.

This paragraph, in addition to its primary significance, gives valuable insight into the position of the Christian as compared to and contrasted with legalists and antinomians. Some Christians, while acknowledging that they have been saved by grace through faith, believe they must live the Christian life as a kind of lawkeeping. Christ saved them, but they must keep themselves saved! This is a form of legalism. As a reaction against that, some other Christians believe that they may live as they please because they are not under law but under grace. They think of the Christian life as essentially lawless. This is known as antinomianism.

Paul made it plain in this passage that he was neither legalistic nor antinomian. He is in an entirely new relationship—not "under the law" and not "lawless," but in a special relationship to Jesus Christ ("in-lawed to Christ").

RUNNING THE RACE (9:24-27)

9:24 Do you not know that those who run in a race all run, but one receives the prize? Run in such a way that you may obtain it.

9:25 And everyone who competes for the prize is temperate in all things. Now they do it to obtain a perishable crown, but we for an imperishable crown.

9:26 Therefore I run thus: not with uncertainty. Thus I fight: not as one who beats the air.

9:27 But I discipline my body and bring it into subjection, lest, when I have preached to others, I myself should become disqualified.

The illustration of a race would have appealed strongly to the Corinthians, who were accustomed to the Isthmian Games every two years. Although not as famous as the Olympic Games, these had been held from dim antiquity and were the topic of much comment among the population. The Greeks emphasized athletics and bodybuilding. They would have known about the discipline required to prepare oneself for the strenuous contests and would have recognized that the prize was a symbol rather than something of intrinsic value. In contrast the apostle saw himself in the race of Christian life and ministry with the reward at the end "an imperishable crown." Just as self-discipline was needed for athletic excellence, so it is doubly needed for Christian living and service.

Paul's allusion to boxing as well as to running emphasizes the strenuous nature of these athletic contests as a parallel to the Christian life. He had to be very careful to control his actions so that he was not simply beating the air, not living ineffectually.

"... I myself should become disqualified." In the context of the epistle and of scripture as a whole, Paul could not have been thinking of losing his salvation (see 1 Corinthians 3:15). The rendering of the KJV ("a castaway") is unfortunate, because it may be wrongly construed as loss of salvation, contrary to the general tenor of scripture. The Greek word is *adokimos*, "disapproved," the negative of *dokimos*, "approved" (2 Timothy 2:15). Paul's concern was that he might lose his usefulness in Christ's service.

OLD TESTAMENT TYPES (10:1-13)

10:1   Moreover, brethren, I do not want you to be unaware that all our fathers were under the cloud, all passed through the sea,

10:2   all were baptized into Moses in the cloud and in the sea,

10:3   all ate the same spiritual food,

10:4   and all drank the same spiritual drink. For they drank of that 'spiritual Rock that followed them, and that Rock was Christ.

10:5   But with most of them God was not well pleased, for their bodies were scattered in the wilderness.

10:6   Now these things became our examples, to the intent that we should not lust after evil things as they also lusted.

10:7   And do not become idolaters as were some of them. As it is written, "The people sat down to eat and drink, and rose up to play."

10:8   Nor let us commit sexual immorality, as some of them did, and in one day twenty-three thousand fell;

10:9   nor let us tempt Christ, as some of them also tempted, and were destroyed by serpents;

10:10 nor complain as some of them also complained, and were destroyed by the destroyer.

10:11 Now all these things happened to them as examples, and they were written for our admonition, upon whom the ends of the ages have come.

10:12 Therefore let him who thinks he stands take heed lest he fall.

10:13 No temptation has overtaken you except such as is

> common to man; but God is faithful, who will not
> allow you to be tempted beyond what you are able,
> but with the temptation will also make the way of
> escape, that you may be able to bear it.

Continuing on in the general subject of Christian liberty, Paul used illustrations from the Old Testament. "I do not want you to be unaware" (KJV, "ignorant"). This is a characteristic expression of Paul, found five times in his epistles (Romans 1:13; 1 Corinthians 10:1; 12:1; 2 Corinthians 1:8; 1 Thessalonians 4:13). It always introduces something of real significance.

The deliverance of Israel from the Egyptians at the Red Sea is often referred to in scripture as a standard and a reminder of God's almighty power. A number of historical psalms recount this outstanding experience (see, for example, Psalm 106:8-9; 136:13-15).

Note the contrast between *all* (five times in 10:1-4) and *most* (10:5). All were brought out of Egypt, but most did not enter the promised land.

The use of the word *baptized* in 10:2, along with the explanatory statement in 12:13, is helpful in our understanding of the term, used here in a figurative or metaphorical sense. Widespread usage from all periods of the Greek language bears out the fact that the key thought in baptism, as the term is used metaphorically, is that of identification. Through the experience at the Red Sea the Israelites were identified with Moses; they were brought under his leadership or influence. That Paul was not speaking here primarily of the ordinance of water baptism, which is a symbol of the reality, is clear in the context, for this is in contrast to his discussion in chapter 1. "By faith they passed through the Red Sea as by dry land" (Hebrews 11:29). None of the Israelites got wet at all, and everyone—including the babies—passed through!

The emphasis is on the universality of the event. All partook of the manna, the heavenly food that God provided (10:3), and all received the refreshing water to drink (cf. Exodus 17:1-7). "That Rock was Christ." Some of the early church fathers believed that the rock from which the water came moved around with the Israelites in their travels. This is not necessary to the understanding of the text. Apparently in most places where they traveled there was sufficient water. Just as God provided essential material water for the thirst of his people, so he provides spiritual water through the Lord Jesus. That rock represents or symbolizes Christ. Verses 6 and 11, in using the word *examples*, exhibit the force of these statements. The Greek word is *typoi*, which has been brought over into English as *types*. A type in this technical sense is a divinely appointed prophetic symbol. Types are found in the Old Testament, principally in the Pentateuch, as indirect prophecies of the coming redeemer. The fulfillment of a type is called an "antitype." All types refer in some way to the Lord Jesus Christ in his person and work. First Corinthians 10 is one of the key New Testament passages on typology (for further extended treatment of this area one should consult the epistle to the Hebrews).

Israel is presented as a warning example to us believers of the present dispensation. Psalm 95 is a commemoration of a number of these experiences of Israel, culminating in the "provocation" in the wilderness (Psalm 95:8 KJV), Israel's unbelief and disobedience at Kadesh-barnea (Numbers 14:1-4).

The quotation in verse 7 is taken from Exodus 32:6, referring to the idolatrous behavior of the people in worshiping the golden calf during Moses' absence on the top of Mt. Sinai. Some have supposed a contradiction between this passage and the account of the sin in the time of Balaam when 24,000 are said to have perished (Numbers 25:9). These are two different events, many years apart. Obviously there can be no contradiction, as Gleason Archer carefully points out in his *Encyclopedia of Bible Difficulties* (page 141). It is interesting to see that the number of those who died after the worship of the golden calf is not recorded in the Old Testament, but is set down here by inspiration. (Note a similar situation in the length of King Saul's reign, mentioned only in Acts 13:21, not in the Old Testament.)

Paul again emphasized that we are to learn from these experiences of Israel and are to heed the warnings of what happened when they disobeyed God. It is possible to be self-deceived and to think that one is capable of withstanding Satan's attacks on one's own. Hence the warning, "Therefore let him who thinks he stands take heed lest he fall" (10:12).

It is not necessary, however, to fall. God has made provision for deliverance. Even though one may think one's trials unique, they are not; they are "common to man." Furthermore, God has limited them to what we can bear because he has provided "the way of escape."

COMMAND TO FLEE FROM IDOLATRY (10:14-22)

10:14 Therefore, my beloved, flee from idolatry.
10:15 I speak as to wise men; judge for yourselves what I say.
10:16 The cup of blessing which we bless, is it not the communion of the blood of Christ? The bread which we break, is it not the communion of the body of Christ?
10:17 For we, though many, are one bread and one body; for we all partake of that one bread.
10:18 Observe Israel after the flesh: Are not those who eat of the sacrifices partakers of the altar?
10:19 What am I saying then? That an idol is anything, or what is offered to idols is anything?
10:20 Rather that the things which the Gentiles sacrifice they sacrifice to demons and not to God, and I do not want you to have fellowship with demons.
10:21 You cannot drink the cup of the Lord and the cup of demons; you cannot partake of the Lord's table and of the table of demons.
10:22 Or do we provoke the Lord to jealousy? Are we stronger than He?

Having warned against entanglement with idolatry from Israel's sad example, the apostle came directly to the point as it pertains to the original question: Is it permissible for believers to partake of a feast in an idol temple? As previously discovered, the answer is in the negative.

Of course, the idol does not really exist; it is a nonentity. That has been conclusively demonstrated. But there is another facet to the problem. Although the idol is nothing, behind the idol stand Satan and his demons. The so-called gods (and goddesses) in the various Greek cults and religions can be traced back to the vast company of evil spirits. Whether aware of this background or not, the Christian who participates in a feast in a pagan temple is in some measure giving credence and even unknowing allegiance to these wicked spirits. Paul called this "fellowship [partnership] with demons."

From this epistle come several terms describing a wonderful ordinance of our Lord: "the communion" (10:16), "the Lord's table" (10:21), and "the Lord's Supper" (11:20).

Very soon Paul was going to explain the significance of the Lord's supper, but at this juncture he connected it with the idea of the one body. As the Lord gave the ordinance (Matthew 26:26-30; Mark 14:22-26; Luke 22:14-23), he used a loaf, which he then broke into pieces for the disciples. He gave the primary significance elsewhere: that it represents the body of Christ given for us on the cross. Here, however, the one loaf is used also to symbolize the unity of all those who belong to Christ through faith in him. In the actual ordinance the bread is mentioned first, then the cup. In the application here the blood is mentioned first, perhaps because of the repeated stress in scripture on our Lord's substitutionary atonement through his shed blood.

LIVING FOR THE GLORY OF GOD (10:23–11:1)

10:23   All things are lawful for me, but not all things are helpful; all things are lawful for me, but not all things edify.

10:24   Let no one seek his own, but each one the other's well-being.

10:25   Eat whatever is sold in the meat market, asking no questions for conscience' sake;

10:26   for "the earth is the LORD'S, and all its fullness."

10:27   If any of those who do not believe invites you to dinner, and you desire to go, eat whatever is set before you, asking no question for conscience' sake.

10:28   But if anyone says to you, "This was offered to idols," do not eat it for the sake of the one who told you, and for conscience' sake; for "the earth is the LORD'S and all its fullness."

10:29   "Conscience," I say, not your own, but that of the other. For why is my liberty judged by another man's conscience?

10:30   But if I partake with thanks, why am I evil spoken of for the food over which I give thanks?

10:31   Therefore, whether you eat or drink, or whatever you do, do all to the glory of God.

10:32 Give no offense, either to the Jews or to the Greeks
or to the church of God.

10:33 Just as I also please all men in all things, not seeking my own profit, but the profit of many, that they
may be saved.

11:1 Imitate me, just as I also imitate Christ.

The "all things" must be understood in this context. Paul obviously was not writing about things definitely condemned in scripture, but was still moving in the realm of the so-called doubtful
matters, those actions that some Christians believe to be wrong
while other Christians see no harm in.

Another interpretation is that an objector was saying to Paul,
"All things are lawful to me," and Paul replied, "But all things are
not helpful."

Enough has been said to reinforce the point that believers
must not participate in idolatrous worship or practices.
Regardless of one's personal beliefs or feelings, others are to be
considered before self (note especially verse 24).

When it comes to the related question of eating meat bought
in the public market, regardless of its origin, the believer is free
to eat and need not ask any questions about its possible relationship to the worship of idols. The sufficient ground given for this
is that the earth belongs to God, who created it (the quotation
being from Psalm 24:1).

The remaining verses of the chapter deal with the third question: Should a believer attend a dinner party in the home of an
unbeliever, and if so, should he inquire about the source of the
meat?

In contrast to the no to question one and the yes to question
two, Paul now gave a maybe, or it depends. Verse 27 states the
general principle. One need not ask any questions. If, however,
someone present does raise the question, then the believer is to
refrain (10:28). Why? On the same ground, that everything
belongs to God (Psalm 24:1) and the believer must not attribute
any of it to an idol.

These instructions have sometimes been broadened and
applied to areas where they are not germane, leaving the impression that the body of believers must give in to the most cantan-
kerous or the least knowledgeable of the saints. It is better, however, to err on the side of giving in than to ignore the views of

others. The summing up of this section on Christian liberty rests on the principles of God's glory (10:31) and men's welfare (10:32). For the former, compare Colossians 3:17.

In the call not to give offense Paul took in the three great ethnic divisions of mankind in God's sight: the Jews, the gentiles (Greeks), and the church. The church is composed of those "called out" from the other two groups.

The first verse of chapter 11 seems to go with that which precedes rather than with the following verses. In carrying out these instructions the Christians will be doing as Paul does.

SUBJECT THREE
Order in the Church
1 Corinthians 11

11:2   Now I praise you, brethren, that you remember me in all things and keep the traditions just as I delivered them to you.

11:3   But I want you to know that the head of every man is Christ, the head of woman is man, and the head of Christ is God.

11:4   Every man praying or prophesying, having his head covered, dishonors his head.

11:5   But every woman who prays or prophesies with her head uncovered dishonors her head, for that is one and the same as if her head were shaved.

11:6   For if a woman is not covered, let her also be shorn. But if it is shameful for a woman to be shorn or shaved, let her be covered.

11:7   For a man indeed ought not to cover his head, since he is the image and glory of God; but woman is the glory of man.

11:8   For man is not from woman, but woman from man.

11:9   Nor was man created for the woman, but woman for the man.

11:10 For this reason the woman ought to have a symbol of authority on her head, because of the angels.

11:11 Nevertheless, neither is man independent of woman, nor woman independent of man, in the Lord.

11:12 For as woman came from man, even so man also comes through woman; but all things are from God.

11:13 Judge among yourselves. Is it proper for a woman
       to pray to God with her head uncovered?
11:14 Does not even nature itself teach you that if a man
       has long hair, it is a dishonor to him?
11:15 But if a woman has long hair, it is a glory to her; for
       her hair is given to her for a covering.
11:16 But if anyone seems to be contentious, we have no
       such custom, nor do the churches of God.

In this section Paul praised the Corinthians for their keeping of
the traditions. This word comes from a root meaning "to hand
down." These are the practices that have been passed on from
the former generation. One of these discussed here is the place
of women in the church; another is the observance of the Lord's
supper (cf. 11:23). In both instances there were areas that
needed correction.

It is clear that God has established order in his universe. Even
among the persons of the godhead there is voluntary subordina-
tion; the Son has subjected himself to the Father's will, for "the
head of Christ is God."

The particular subject discussed here is the attitude and attire
of women in the public worship services of the church. The praying and prophesying mentioned are clearly a part of public ministry. As always, scripture should be compared with scripture.
The instructions in 14:34-35 must be considered in connection
with this passage and also with 1 Timothy 2:11-15.

However one interprets the parallel passages, this section does
recognize some part by women in the public services. There
were some prophetesses in Old Testament times (e.g., Miriam in
Exodus 15:20, Deborah in Judges 4:4, Huldah in 2 Kings 22:14);
and there were some in the New Testament (the four daughters
of Philip the evangelist were specifically so described in Acts
21:8-9). In this context Paul was not questioning whether women
should pray or prophesy, but how they should do it while maintaining the place God has given them in the church.

An expression that is overworked and often misused is "cul-
turally conditioned." Perhaps, however, the expression fits here.
In the culture of the first century honorable women wore veils
when in public places and situations. It seems that prostitutes
and other immoral women appeared without such a covering. A
woman who would participate in the worship of the church with-

out the customary covering would seem to be open to being mis-understood and misjudged.

Although the subject of the relationship of the sexes is an extremely complicated one, it is clear in scripture that God established an order in the creation and that headship was committed to the man. In the church there should be a recognition of that order; this was customarily shown by a woman wearing a head-covering.

In verse 10 the translators have inserted the words "a symbol of" to clarify the thought, but the most difficult part of the statement is in the words "because of the angels." Some take this to be a reference to the pastor or human messenger in the church who might be distracted from his message by the women who did not conform to the tradition of a covering, but this seems far-fetched, even though the Greek word is often used of human messengers and is probably so used in Revelation 1:20.

It is more likely that Paul was referring to the fact that angels, as beings who are completely subject to the will of God and who are eagerly observing what is going on among the people of God (cf. 1 Peter 1:12), are pleased and helped in their worship of God by seeing human beings living in conformity to his will.

Paul was evidently arguing from the prevailing customs and using the word *nature* to designate these (11:14). The word *covering* seems somewhat ambiguous, for in verse 15 the apostle spoke of the woman's long hair as a *covering*. Verse 16 is our authority for believing that this passage is stating a principle, not a binding commandment.

PROPER OBSERVANCE OF THE LORD'S SUPPER (11:17-22)

11:17 Now in giving these instructions I do not praise you, since you come together not for the better but for the worse.

11:18 For first of all, when you come together as a church, I hear that there are divisions among you, and in part I believe it.

11:19 For there must also be factions among you, that those who are approved may be recognized among you.

11:20 Therefore when you come together in one place, it is not to eat the Lord's Supper.

11:21   For in eating, each one takes his own supper ahead
        of others; and one is hungry and another is drunk.
11:22   What! Do you not have houses to eat and drink in?
        Or do you despise the church of God and shame
        those who have nothing? What shall I say to you?
        Shall I praise you in this? I do not praise you.

Note the contrast between verse 2 on the one hand and verses
17 and 22 on the other. In one instance the apostle praised, in the
other he emphatically did not. In the case of the Lord's supper
he did not accept variations as a matter of indifference. This is
one of the two special ordinances the Lord Jesus has given to his
church. The Corinthians were making a mockery of this ordinance, as they did also of the ordinance of baptism by claiming
to be identified with human leaders. They were carrying their differences into the sacred meetings of the church when they
should have been assembled to show their unity and their faith
in Christ alone by partaking of the Lord's supper.

Regardless of what they were claiming, Paul stated, they were
not really coming together to observe the ordinance. They were
confusing it with a common meal in which they were not sharing
with those who had nothing of their own. That which should
have been a unifying experience became a point of division
instead. Alongside the hunger of some who had no food was
seen the actual drunkenness of some others. Scripture is
unsparing in its condemnation of drunkenness (e.g., Proverbs
20:1; 23:31-35). The apostle's instructions showed that the
Corinthians were not to confuse the ordinance with an ordinary
meal. The *agape* or love feast in connection with the supper was
evidently well intentioned, but subject to abuse. Therefore it
was not to be combined with the God-given ordinance.

THE WORDS OF INSTITUTION OF THE LORD'S SUPPER (11:23-26)

11:23   For I received from the Lord that which I also deliv-
        ered to you: that the Lord Jesus on the same night
        in which He was betrayed took bread;
11:24   and when He had given thanks, He broke it and said,
        "Take, eat; this is My body which is broken for you;
        do this in remembrance of Me."
11:25   In the same manner He also took the cup after sup-

per, saying, "This cup is the new covenant in My blood. This do, as often as you drink it, in remembrance of Me."

11:26 For as often as you eat this bread and drink this cup, you proclaim the Lord's death till He comes.

When and where did Paul receive from the Lord the word concerning this ordinance? He was not present, of course, in the upper room when the Lord instituted the supper (Matthew 26:26-30; Mark 14:22-26; Luke 22:14-23). No doubt he had received this along with the other teachings which the Lord gave to him personally as a part of his apostleship (cf. 9:1, along with Galatians 1:11-12). When he said he "received [it] from the Lord," he meant that there were no intermediaries. This was a direct revelation from Jesus Christ.

Endless controversy surrounds the two ordinances given by Christ to his church: baptism and the Lord's supper. The former is discussed in connection with the next chapter (12:13). The controversy around the Lord's supper involves the affirmation or the denial of what is called theologically the "real presence" of Christ. This is connected also with the idea that arose in the church of the ordinances as "sacraments," that is, as mysteries which impart special grace to those who partake. Historically, the major views of the Lord's supper are four in number:

First, that the bread and wine are actually transformed into the real body and blood of Christ at the words of institution by a priest: *"Hoc est corpus meum"* ("This is My body"). This view is known historically as *transubstantiation*. It is the view taught by the Roman Catholic Church.

Second, that the body and the blood of Christ are literally present "in, with and under" the elements of bread and wine, although the elements remain unchanged. This is the view of Martin Luther; it is known technically as *consubstantiation*. Both of these views involve the idea of the "real presence." In both of them the partaker is said to be the recipient of special grace through physically partaking of the elements.

Third, that the body and blood of Christ are not physically, but spiritually, present at the Lord's supper and that through faith the partaker receives spiritual benefit. This is the view of John Calvin.

Fourth, that the Lord's supper is a simple memorial of which believers partake as they remember what the Lord Jesus has done for them by his death on the cross. No special grace is imparted by the elements as such, but the believing partaker is strengthened and edified as he remembers his Lord in his person and his atoning work. This was the view of Huldrych Zwingli, the Swiss reformer. It seems to be closest to scripture. Historically many Calvinists seem to have followed Zwingli rather than Calvin in their interpretation of the Lord's supper. If one takes the simple words of the Lord as given in scripture, this seems to be the plain meaning. When he instituted the supper he was holding the bread before them. When he said, "This is My body," they could see that he was present with them in his literal body; obviously the bread was distinct from that. One who approaches this from the viewpoint of the Bible, having stripped away all the theological and historical accretions, can see that the word *is* is being used here in a way it is commonly used: "This *represents* My body."

This is further borne out by the fact that the word *wine* is never used in the descriptions of the ordinance; it is always "the cup" or "this cup." If anything becomes literally changed into the blood of Christ it would have to be the literal cup since nothing is said about the literal contents, and the word *cup* is the exact parallel of the word *bread* or *loaf*.

The ordinances are never seen in scripture as a means of salvation. The believer who partakes of the Lord's supper is using the ordinance as a blessed reminder of what the Lord Jesus did for him.

Verse 26 has often been characterized as describing the Lord's supper as a great bridge spanning this present age. Every time we partake we look back in loving remembrance of what he did, but we also look forward in keen anticipation of his return in fulfillment of his promise (John 14:2-3).

Edward Bickersteth's great hymn (1862) expresses this thought beautifully:

> "Till He come!" O let the words
>   Linger on the trembling chords;
> Let the little while between
>   In their golden light be seen;
> Let us think how heaven and home
>   Lie beyond that "Till He come!"

See, the feast of love is spread,
   Drink the wine, and break the bread;
Sweet memorials,— till the Lord
   Call us round His heavenly board;
Some from earth, from glory some,
   Severed only "Till He come!"

There is no commandment in scripture regulating the frequency of the ordinance. It seems probable that the early Christians observed it every Lord's day (the first day of the week; cf. Acts 20:7, where there is some uncertainty whether the expression "to break bread" refers to the Lord's supper or to an ordinary meal).

OBSERVING WORTHILY OR UNWORTHILY (11:27-34)

11:27 Therefore whoever eats this bread or drinks this cup of the Lord in an unworthy manner will be guilty of the body and blood of the Lord.
11:28 But let a man examine himself, and so let him eat of the bread and drink of the cup.
11:29 For he who eats and drinks in an unworthy manner eats and drinks judgment to himself, not discerning the Lord's body.
11:30 For this reason many are weak and sick among you, and many sleep.
11:31 For if we would judge ourselves, we would not be judged.
11:32 But when we are judged, we are chastened by the Lord, that we may not be condemned with the world.
11:33 Therefore, my brethren, when you come together to eat, wait for one another.
11:34 But if anyone is hungry, let him eat at home, lest you come together for judgment. And the rest I will set in order when I come.

Distinction must be made between being unworthy and doing something unworthily or in an unworthy manner. We are all unworthy in the sense of undeserving of God's mercies. Grace, as we have seen, is essentially undeserved, unearned, and unrecompensed. If one were to wait to partake until he were worthy, he would never partake. As one famous *Book of Common Worship* states: "All that humbly put their trust in Christ, and desire His help that they may lead a holy life, all that are truly sorry for their sins and would be delivered from the burden of them, are invited and encouraged in His Name to come."

To partake unworthily or in an unworthy manner is to receive the elements without regard to their significance, to take them thoughtlessly or flippantly. A person is pronounced "guilty of the body and blood of the Lord" because he has not understood that this solemnly and beautifully represents in pictorial form what the Lord Jesus accomplished for us through his substitutionary death on the cross of Calvary.

The Lord's supper is an occasion of self-examination—not that true believers should abstain, for the text says, "But let a man examine himself, and so let him eat. . . ." Three kinds of judgment are mentioned in the passage.

First is the believer's self-judgment, in which he confesses his sin and turns from it (cf. 1 John 1:9).

Second is God's chastening, which he brings on his children who refuse to judge themselves. In severe instances this judgment leads to illness and even to physical death (11:30; cf. 1 John 5:16). Needless to say, we must be extremely cautious about passing judgment on the reasons for the death of believers and professed believers. The seemingly premature death of a believer may have no relationship to the observance of the Lord's supper. That is something completely in God's control.

Third is God's condemnation of the world (11:32).

The KJV translation "damnation" in verse 29 is confusing to many modern readers because that word is thought of in connection with eternal condemnation. The word *judgment* is the better term here.

The early church questioned whether the prevailing note in the Lord's supper should be joy or sorrow. The answer is that both emotions are mingled. Godly sorrow for sin and true joy in the Lord go together.

SUBJECT FOUR
Spiritual Gifts
1 Corinthians 12–14

VARIOUS GIFTS FROM THE SAME HOLY SPIRIT (12:1-11))

12:1   Now concerning spiritual gifts, brethren, I do not want you to be ignoant:

12:2   You know that you were Gentiles, carried away to these dumb idols, however you were led.

12:3   Therefore I make known to you that no one speaking by the Spirit of God calls Jesus accursed, and no one can say that Jesus is Lord except by the Holy Spirit.

12:4   There are diversities of gifts, but the same Spirit.

12:5   There are differences of ministries, but the same Lord.

12:6   And there are diversities of activities, but it is the same God who works all in all.

12:7   But the manifestation of the Spirit is given to each one for the profit of all:

12:8   for to one is given the word of wisdom through the Spirit, to another the word of knowledge through the same Spirit,

12:9   to another faith by the same Spirit, to another gifts of healings by the same Spirit,

12:10 to another the working of miracles, to another prophecy, to another discerning of spirits, to another different kinds of tongues, to another the interpretation of tongues.

12:11 But one and the same Spirit works all these things, distributing to each one individually as He wills.

In chapters 12 through 14 the apostle dealt with the broad area of spiritual gifts. In 1 Corinthians 12 and Romans 12 he compared the whole company of believers as the body of Christ to the human body, in which the different members and organs, although so diverse, function together in a harmonious whole. In these passages certain gifts, which the Holy Spirit gives to individuals, are described and differentiated. In a parallel passage in Ephesians 4 Paul wrote of men with differing offices and abilities whom the Holy Spirit gives to the church for the work of the ministry as performed by the whole body.

The twentieth century has witnessed many claims to supernatural gifts of various kinds. The "pentecostal" movement in the early years of the century led to the founding of numerous denominations seeking to emulate the first-century pattern. Again, in the latter third of the century, the so-called "charismatic movement" has won many adherents in old-line Protestant denominations and even in the Roman Catholic Church. The teaching, therefore, of this section is of great significance at the present hour.

One of the important questions concerns whether the so-called sign gifts (such as tongues and healing, especially) are for the whole church age or only for the beginning of the church's history. First Corinthians is unique in that it is the only epistle which mentions the gift of tongues. Some of the questions, then, are: What is the gift of tongues? Is the gift of tongues in 1 Corinthians the same as speaking in tongues in the book of Acts? Are this gift and other sign gifts for this whole age?

This commentary takes the position that the "tongues" in the book of Acts are real languages, not some sort of "heavenly utterance"; that the tongues in 1 Corinthians are the same as in Acts, although the Corinthians were abusing the gift; that some of the gifts in the early church, including the gift of tongues, were temporary and, in fact, were ceasing even in the first century; and that the sign gifts were for evidence and confirmation of the message that was being preached. As the canon of the New Testament was formed, and ultimately completed and closed with the book of Revelation, the need for the sign gifts ceased. Although God is a miracle-working God and can do anything he pleases whenever he pleases, the evidence is clear that even in the Old Testament times there were special periods of miracles in Israel's history. These were: first, the period of the exodus and the wilderness wanderings; and second, the time of deepest apostasy in the two kingdoms (especially Israel, the northern kingdom), which was the period of the outstanding prophets, Elijah and Elisha.

Coming into the New Testament we can add the third and greatest period, the time of the Lord Jesus Christ and the apostles. The Lord Jesus worked mighty miracles as his credentials, as prophesied in the Old Testament (see, for example, Isaiah 35). The apostles and other early witnesses were often given miraculous gifts to display along with the gospel message. This is summed up in Mark 16:14-20, which many interpreters today do not accept as genuine (but see John William Burgon, *The Last Twelve Verses of St. Mark*, 1959 reprint, edited by Edward F. Hills). Hebrews 2:1-4 is not a doubtful passage textually and it confirms the same truth.

Two other passages which attest the temporary nature of some of the gifts are Ephesians 4:7-16 and 1 Corinthians 13:8-13.

The passage in Ephesians 4 mentions different kinds of men whom God gave as gifts to the church for the purpose of equipping the whole church for the work of ministry. The first group in the list were "apostles." From a number of passages, including the attacks on Paul as though he were not an apostle, it can be seen that the gift of apostleship was temporary in the church (note Ephesians 2:20, where the apostles were said to be the "foundation," not the superstructure). The apostles were directly commissioned by the Lord himself and had no successors. After the death of the apostle John at the close of the first century, there were no more apostles.

Similarly, the office of "prophet" was a temporary one in the church. A prophet, beginning in Old Testament times, was a spokesperson for God, one who received a direct revelation from God and passed it on to the people. Paul classified himself as both an apostle (note his claims in his various epistles) and a prophet (as has been shown above). Here again the special need for that gift ceased with the completion of the canon of scripture. God is not giving new revelations today, but the Holy Spirit is illuminating scripture, the revelation already given, so that his people can understand it.

The passage in Hebrews 2 tells how some in the first generation of Christian witnesses had their testimony confirmed by miraculous sign gifts. The writer seemed to distinguish between that generation and his own—"confirmed to us by those who heard Him" (2:3); the implication is that those gifts were of a temporary nature.

In 1 Corinthians 12:1 the translators have inserted the word *gifts* on the authority of verse 4. This is logical and correct. The familiar "now concerning" shows that the Corinthians in their letter had asked Paul about spiritual gifts. The principal difficulty in this area seems to have been a misunderstanding and misuse of one of the gifts, that of tongues or languages.

Before dealing with individual gifts, Paul emphasized that the Holy Spirit of God is the sovereign giver and distributor of all spiritual gifts. He stressed the significance of what he was about to write by using his formula, "I do not want you to be ignorant." It is as though he were saying, This is very important to know; therefore, pay close attention to what I am writing.

Reminding them of their background before they knew the Lord Jesus Christ, he contrasted their former position as "Gentiles" and those "carried away to these dumb [mute or unspeaking] idols" with their new and present position. They had received the Holy Spirit, as he was shortly to emphasize and explain further. The very fact that they were for the Lord Jesus Christ instead of against him, and that they acknowledged him as Lord, is conclusive evidence that they knew and had the Holy Spirit.

The passage teaches the unity of all believers which has been worked in them and for them by the Holy Spirit, a truth to be further developed in the next paragraph. The overall thought is of unity in diversity or diversity in unity. The Holy Spirit has been given to each believer and he is the ground of this unity. As so often in scripture, there are intimations of the trinity, the one God existing in three persons. Here the order is the reverse of the usual, with the Holy Spirit being mentioned first, because he is the person of the godhead who has the responsibility for the distribution of the spiritual gifts (cf. Ephesians 4:1-6, a true parallel).

"The same Spirit," "the same Lord," "the same God." We are reminded of a line from that great hymn of the faith, written by Reginald Heber, "God in three Persons, blessed Trinity!"

All do not have the same gifts (12:4); therefore, it is unscriptural to insist that every Christian must have a particular gift (such as tongues) as an evidence of the "baptism" of the Holy Spirit. Much of the confusion in the church today about the gifts of the Spirit comes from confusing the baptism of the Holy Spirit with the filling of the Holy Spirit and further confusing both of these ministries with the gifts of the Holy Spirit (the particular subject in these immediate verses).

Beginning with verse 8 the apostle showed that some have a certain gift or gifts and others have another gift or other gifts. The summation in verse 11 insists that the Holy Spirit is sovereign in giving the gifts; that is, he does not have to follow a man-appointed order or schedule, but he does as he pleases.

MEMBERS AND FUNCTIONS OF THE ONE BODY (12:12-31)

12:12 For as the body is one and has many members, but all the members of that one body, being many, are one body, so also is Christ.

12:13 For by one Spirit we were all baptized into one body—whether Jews or Greeks, whether slaves or free—and have all been made to drink into one Spirit.

12:14 For in fact the body is not one member but many.

12:15 If the foot should say, "Because I am not a hand, I am not of the body," is it therefore not of the body?

12:16 And if the ear should say, "Because I am not an eye, I am not of the body," is it therefore not of the body?

12:17 If the whole body were an eye, where would be the hearing? If the whole were hearing, where would be the smelling?

12:18 But now God has set the members, each one of them, in the body just as He pleased.

12:19 And if they were all one member, where would the body be?

12:20 But now indeed there are many members, yet one body.

12:21 And the eye cannot say to the hand, "I have no need of you"; nor again the head to the feet, "I have no need of you."

12:22 No, much rather, those members of the body which seem to be weaker are necessary.

12:23 And those members of the body which we think to be less honorable, on these we bestow greater

> honor; and our unpresentable parts have greater modesty,
>
> 12:24 but our presentable parts have no need. But God composed the body, having given greater honor to that part which lacks it,
>
> 12:25 that there should be no schism in the body, but that the members should have the same care for one another.
>
> 12:26 And if one member suffers, all the members suffer with it; or if one member is honored, all the members rejoice with it.
>
> 12:27 Now you are the body of Christ, and members individually.
>
> 12:28 And God has appointed these in the church: first apostles, second prophets, third teachers, after that miracles, then gifts of healings, helps, administrations, varieties of tongues.
>
> 12:29 Are all apostles? Are all prophets? Are all teachers? Are all workers of miracles?
>
> 12:30 Do all have gifts of healings? Do all speak with tongues? Do all interpret?
>
> 12:31 But earnestly desire the best gifts. And yet I show you a more excellent way.

A reason that the Holy Spirit distributes as he wants to is that the one body of Christ, made up of all true believers, is so diverse. Not everyone has all the gifts or the same particular gift as everyone else because not everyone needs the same gift or gifts. There is a beautiful and orderly arrangement in the body just as in the healthily functioning human body.

The doctrine of the baptism of the Holy Spirit, which is developed here, is often greatly misunderstood. It is announced in the gospels as something to be activated by the Lord Jesus (see Matthew 3:11; Mark 1:4-8; Luke 3:16-17). At the close of the Lord's earthly ministry he promised the disciples that the baptism of the Holy Spirit, which still had not occurred, would soon begin (Acts 1:4-5).

Scripture shows that there are four ministries of the Holy Spirit in this age which involve all believers. Since the day of Pentecost (Acts 2) these all occur instantaneously and simultaneously. They are the Holy Spirit's regenerating, indwelling, baptizing, and sealing ministries. No believer is ever commanded in the New Testament to be regenerated by the Holy Spirit; he is informed that he was regenerated by the Holy Spirit the moment he believed in the Lord Jesus Christ (Titus 3:4-7; 1 Peter 1:22-25).

The same thing can be said concerning the indwelling and sealing ministries (John 14:16-17; Ephesians 1:13-14; 4:30). The Holy Spirit has come into the life of the believer and will never leave. Furthermore, since he has come to stay, his presence is the guarantee that our salvation will one day be complete, even to the resurrection of our body (Romans 8:23).

Not all agree that the baptizing ministry is in the same category as the three ministries just mentioned. In the present text, however, the statement is made that "we were all baptized into one body" (12:13). "We all" in Paul's language means all of us believers in the Lord Jesus Christ; not some believers, but "all"; not someday will be, but "have been"; not to seek the baptism, but to recognize it. This ministry promised by our Lord shortly before he ascended to heaven began on the day of Pentecost when the Holy Spirit formed the individual believers into the one body of Christ. Since that time each new believer has been placed into the body when he believes. It is true that the Holy Spirit also filled the disciples when he came upon them on the day of Pentecost (Acts 2:4) and that he also granted to them the gift of tongues. This gift was for a special reason on that occasion: in order that each person present might hear the glad tidings in his own language, his "mother-tongue" (Acts 2:5-11). The fact that at this particular time the Holy Spirit did at least three things in the lives of those believers does not cause the ministries of baptizing and filling to be identical, nor does it identify the gift of tongues with those ministries.

Our English versions generally recognize the difficulties in the Greek word *baptizein*, and for that reason usually simply transliterate the Greek word into the English text. It is commonly held that the word means "to dip," but there is a regular Greek word meaning to dip (*bapto*), which occurs in only a few places in the New Testament (Luke 16:24; John 13:26; Revelation 19:13).

Baptizein and its noun counterparts were used in the time of the New Testament to indicate cleansing, without reference to the mode (note, for example, Mark 7:4,8; Hebrews 9:10). The usage in Hebrews has to do with Old Testament ritual cleansings, some of which were by pouring or sprinkling. The word took on the figurative or metaphorical significance of identification, as mentioned previously.

One of the most thorough treatments of this difficult subject was that by James W. Dale a century ago, particularly in his book, *Christic and Patristic Baptism*. He wrote (page 17):

> REAL Christic baptism is a thorough change in the moral condition of the soul effected by the Holy Ghost and uniting to Christ by repentance and faith, and through Christ re-establishing filial and everlasting relation with the living God—Father, Son and Holy Ghost. RITUAL Christic baptism is not another and diverse baptism, but is one and the same baptism declared by word, and exhibited (as to its purifying nature) by pure water applied to the body; symbolizing the cleansing of the soul through the atoning blood of Christ by the Holy Ghost.

The analogy of the body of Christ and the human body is carried out in some detail. There is stress on the combination of unity and diversity, the one and the many. Within the array of different members are differences of function as well as of form. One part can do what another part cannot; therefore, one part ought not to pride itself above others, and conversely, it should not feel inferior because of being different (cf. Romans 14).

The amazing grace and condescension of the Lord Jesus Christ is portrayed in the introductory statement of verse 12: "So also is [the] Christ." Astoundingly, the whole body—not just the head—is called "[the] Christ." Every member partakes of the honor rightfully belonging to the head.

There are a number of figures or metaphors in the New Testament to describe the relationship of Christ and the church (e.g., the shepherd and the sheep in John 10, the vine and the branches in John 15, the great high priest and the royal priesthood in 1 Peter 2, the chief cornerstone and the stones of the temple in Ephesians 2 and 1 Peter 2, the last Adam and the new creation in Romans 5 and 1 Corinthians 15, and the bridegroom and the bride in 2 Corinthians 11:2 and Revelation 21). While this description may also be called a metaphor, it expresses a transcendent reality. Each believer is just as really and fully joined spiritually to the Lord Jesus Christ as any part of the human body is joined physically to the rest of the body. There is a common life permeating and penetrating the whole body from the blessed head.

Because the church is a body in this sense, every individual member has a function to perform, a unique place to fill. At the close of this section Paul enumerated some of the gifts that the Holy Spirit has bestowed on the church (cf. Ephesians 4).

"First apostles . . ." The office of apostle was limited in number and in time. The apostles belonged to the first century, to the first generation of the church. They, along with the prophets, are said to comprise the "foundation" (Ephesians 2; see above).

Teachers are more numerous and are found throughout the church's history. Although the apostles and prophets had no successors, the noble line of teachers continues down through the centuries. Yet scripture is clear that those who hold these sacred offices and exercise these God-given gifts are to wait on him for their instruction and enablement (cf. James 3:1).

The questions in verses 29 and 30 require a negative answer; the Greek is absolutely clear on that: "All are not apostles, are they?" (The answer is no.) "All are not prophets, are they?" (The answer is no.) And so on. The most controversial of these gifts seem to be healing and tongues (languages). Of course, all do not have the gifts of healing. Paul himself had a gift of healing, but did not or could not always use it ("Trophimus I have left at Miletum sick" [2 Timothy 4:20]), not even for his own benefit (2 Corinthians 12:9-10).

The gift of tongues and the gift of interpretation are placed last in this list, another indication that these are not universal gifts bestowed on all true believers. The Greek word translated "tongues" means literally "languages." There is no indication in scripture that tongues meant a secret kind of ecstatic utterance, a "heavenly language."

The description of the "best gifts" is given in chapter 14. But in the meantime the apostle showed what he meant by the "more excellent way."

THE SUPREMACY OF LOVE (13:1-13)

13:1   Though I speak with the tongues of men and of
        angels, but have not love, I have become sounding
        brass or a clanging cymbal.

13:2   And though I have the gift of prophecy, and under-
       stand all mysteries and all knowledge, and though
       I have all faith, so that I could remove mountains,
       but have not love, I am nothing.

13:3   And though I bestow all my goods to feed the poor,
       and though I give my body to be burned, but have
       not love, it profits me nothing.

13:4   Love suffers long and is kind; love does not envy;
       love does not parade itself, is not puffed up;

13:5   does not behave rudely, does not seek its own, is
       not provoked, thinks no evil;

13:6   does not rejoice in iniquity, but rejoices in the
       truth;

13:7   bears all things, believes all things, hopes all things,
       endures all things.

13:8   Love never fails. But whether there are prophe-
       cies, they will fail; whether there are tongues, they
       will cease; whether there is knowledge, it will van-
       ish away.

13:9   For we know in part and we prophesy in part.

13:10 But when that which is perfect has come, then that
       which is in part will be done away.

13:11 When I was a child, I spoke as a child, I understood
       as a child, I thought as a child; but when I became
       a man, I put away childish things.

13:12 For now we see in a mirror, dimly, but then face to
       face. Now I know in part, but then I shall know
       just as I also am known.

13:13 And now abide faith, hope, love, these three; but
       the greatest of these is love.

This section obviously is the "more excellent way" just mentioned by the apostle. Unless the gifts are administered in love,
they are without real significance. The chapter can be outlined
as follows:

(1) The Indispensability of Love (13:1-3);
(2) The Nature of Love (13:4-7);
(3) The Eternity of Love (13:8-13).

The Indispensability of Love

No matter what kind or how many languages one can speak as a supernatural gift from the Spirit of God, all are meaningless apart from love. "Sounding brass" and "clanging cymbal" make loud noises, but afford no meaning. A famous kind of loud gong was manufactured in Corinth (Murphy-O'Connor, *St. Paul's Corinth*).

The gift of prophecy, which Paul was to describe as of major importance (14:1), is valueless without love. Even faith which is essential for salvation—and not only bare faith, but extraordinary faith ("so that I could remove mountains," see Matthew 17:20)—is without efficacy unless exercised with benevolence and kindness as an expression of love.

Extreme self-sacrifice and even martyrdom, strange as this may seem, may be an outflow from an unloving spirit, and thus profitless.

The Nature of Love

It has often been remarked that love as described here is a perfect picture of the character of the Lord Jesus Christ. The human tendency is to be unkind, especially after manifesting longsuffering as indicated here. True love continues to be kind after the most extreme form of endurance. Conversely, the old human nature manifests itself in ways contrary to this description. The list of what love does and does not do can be compared to the enumeration of the works of the flesh and the elements contained in the "fruit of the Spirit" in Galatians 5:16-24.

Most of these qualities are self-explanatory. "Believes all things" (13:7) does not mean that love is gullible or credulous, so naive as to believe every foolish thing that anybody says. It refers rather to that loving attitude which wants to believe the best about anyone and which will only reluctantly change its attitude if forced to do so.

Love in scripture is not a mere emotion, but a volitional decision actively to desire and to seek the welfare of another. Contrary to the world's idea, which is self-centered and grasping, true divine love, as described in the Bible, is centered on the one loved, and is outgoing and giving.

The Eternity of Love

Love goes on and on. Prophecies will "fail," not in the sense that they will be proved wrong, but that they will be fulfilled and will no longer be necessary.

"Whether there are tongues, they will cease." There are two major interpretations of this statement. It may mean that languages as such will come to an end, blended into the one final, complete language—a counterpart to the one language that all men spoke before the building of the tower of Babel (Genesis 11:1).

Another possibility is that the gift of tongues or languages was to cease on completion of the canon of scripture, as the other sign gifts also were to cease (cf. Hebrews 2:1-3). It is doubtful that anyone has the gift of tongues today in the sense in which the term is used in scripture. When we think of the many dedicated servants of the Lord Jesus Christ today who are laboriously learning difficult languages in order to give the gospel to those who speak those languages, we might ask, "If God is giving the gift of tongues today, why doesn't he give it to those who have the greatest need for it?"

The catalog of Moody Bible Institute contains a "Statement on the Modern Tongues-Speaking Movement" which is germane and helpful, pointing out that the movement "usually gives an undue prominence to a gift that had only limited value even in New Testament times (1 Corinthians 12–14)" and that "it often suggests that tongues-speaking is the necessary evidence of the special work of the Spirit when in fact the New Testament does not say this" (page 7).

Knowledge "will vanish away"—not that we shall lose all the knowledge which we have had, but that experience will lead to greater knowledge, which will supersede our previous knowledge. Verse 9 is explanatory of verse 8.

Verse 10 is the crux of interpretation of the passage. Is this referring to the future eternity or to the completion of the canon of scripture? Probably the former, following the analogy of verse 12. The apostle could hardly say that when the canon was complete, he would have the full knowledge which he does not now possess.

Mirrors in the first century were not as bright and clear as those of today. Usually made of burnished metal, they did not give a perfect image. The word "dimly" can be translated "in a riddle" or "in an enigma." A time is coming ultimately when there will be no need for the gift of tongues, the gift of knowledge, or even the gift of prophecy. Then the eternally abiding qualities will be recognized as superior to even the sign gifts.

Paul listed faith, hope, and love as those qualities that will remain long after the need for the miraculous gifts, which attested to the truth of the gospel in the foundation time of the church.

Why is love characterized as the greatest of the abiding qualities? Some have said, because love alone lasts forever, but that is a misreading of the text. According to Greek grammatical style a singular verb is used, but this verb is to be construed with each part of the compound subject. NKJV makes this clear, as do also NIV and NASB.

Love is the greatest of these qualities because it is the only one of the three that is an attribute of God. God does not exercise faith, because there is no one in whom he could have faith. He is the supreme object of faith. It is the responsibility of creatures to have faith in their creator. Faith implies dependence. The redeemed of the Lord will trust him throughout all eternity. Even though sight will have come, God's people will always need to trust him. It will not require any effort on the part of the completely redeemed to trust God, but nevertheless they will trust him.

It is similar with hope. Hope in scripture is the absolute certainty of future good. Scripture seems to indicate that there will always be a sequence of events for saved people even in heaven,because we shall never be infinite. God is the only infinite being. For him all eternity is an eternal now, but for us the endless ages will unfold in succession. The strongest way of expressing eternity in the Greek New Testament is by the phrase, "the ages of the ages." We shall know that there is always some blessing ahead. Our hope is in God. But God himself does not exercise hope, nor will he ever need to.

But the Bible says, "God is love" (1 John 4:8,16). Love is one of the eternal moral attributes of God. It so characterizes him that it can properly be placed as the predicate nominative in a statement about him, equating the predicate with the subject. Note that this is an irreversible proposition. The subject and the predicate nominative cannot be interchanged. The Greek grammar is perfectly clear, for when two nouns in the nominative case are joined by a form of the verb *to be*, and only one has the definite article, the noun with the article is, and must be, the subject regardless of the word order in the Greek sentence. Note John 1:1: "The Word [articular] was God [anarthrous]". It could never be reversed. To say, "God was the Word," would not be accurate. For a truly reversible proposition, see 1 John 3:4: "[The] sin is [the] lawlessness." It would be just as true and just as accurate to say, "Lawlessness is sin," for each noun has the article.

Scripture never says that God is faith; it says, "Have faith in God" (Mark 11:22). It never says that God is hope; it says that our hope is in God (1 Peter 1:21). But it does say emphatically that "God is love" (1 John 4:8,16). As an attribute of God himself, love is communicable to his creatures. "We love Him because He first loved us" (1 John 4:19). When we exercise the kind of love described and imparted in the Bible, we are manifesting God's own love bestowed on us and working through us to reach others.

The translators of KJV evidently wanted to use a more exalted and unusual word for this eternal quality. Therefore, they used the word *charity*, from the Latin *charitas*, not "charity" in our modern sense of the term. The Greek word is *agape*, as in many other passages; e.g., 1 John where KJV translates *love* in scores of instances. In current English usage *love* is more understandable and more accurate than *charity*.

PROPHECY AND TONGUES COMPARED AND CONTRASTED (14:1-5)

14:1 Pursue love, and desire spiritual gifts, but especially that you may prophesy.

14:2 For he who speaks in a tongue does not speak to men but to God, for no one understands him; however, in the spirit he speaks mysteries.

14:3 But he who prophesies speaks edification and exhortation and comfort to men.

14:4 He who speaks in a tongue edifies himself, but he who prophesies edifies the church.

14:5 I wish you all spoke with tongues, but even more that you prophesied; for he who prophesies is greater than he who speaks with tongues, unless indeed he interprets, that the church may receive edification.

Note the close connection between the end of chapter 13 and the beginning of chapter 14. Regardless of the presence or absence of spiritual gifts, we are commanded to "pursue love." And certainly spiritual gifts are not to be despised or ignored. It is proper, Paul said, to desire them. At the outset of this paragraph, however, he was careful to assess the relative importance of the gifts and to show the primacy of prophesying. This does not mean merely expounding or explaining scripture. It means to transmit new revelations from God. In this respect the New Testament prophets were like the Old Testament prophets. We have seen previously that prophets are classified along with apostles as the "foundation" of the church. This shows that the office had to do with the beginning of the church's ministry, not its entire history.

The gift of tongues, without the gift of interpretation, leaves the recipient of the gift unable to communicate a meaningful message, for even he does not know what he is saying. "No one understands him."

Some of the Corinthians, by misusing the gift of tongues, were drawing attention to themselves rather than to the Lord. Although they might have found the experience edifying to themselves, they were not helping others, because no one could understand what they were saying.

NECESSITY OF THE INTERPRETATION OF TONGUES (14:6-19)

14:6　But now, brethren, if I come to you speaking with tongues, what shall I profit you unless I speak to you either by revelation, by knowledge, by prophesying, or by teaching?

14:7　Even things without life, whether flute or harp, when they make a sound, unless they make a distinction in the sounds, how will it be known what is piped or played?

14:8　For if the trumpet makes an uncertain sound, who will prepare for battle?

14:9　So likewise you, unless you utter by the tongue words easy to understand, how will it be known what is spoken? For you will be speaking into the air.

14:10　There are, it may be, so many kinds of languages

in the world, and none of them is without significance.

14:11 Therefore, if I do not know the meaning of the language, I shall be a foreigner to him who speaks, and he who speaks will be a foreigner to me.

14:12 Even so you, since you are zealous for spiritual gifts, let it be for the edification of the church that you seek to excel.

14:13 Therefore let him who speaks in a tongue pray that he may interpret.

14:14 For if I pray in a tongue, my spirit prays, but my understanding is unfruitful.

14:15 What is the conclusion then? I will pray with the spirit, and I will also pray with the understanding. I will sing with the spirit, and I will also sing with the understanding.

14:16 Otherwise, if you bless with the spirit, how will he who occupies the place of the uninformed say "Amen" at your giving of thanks, since he does not understand what you say?

14:17 For you indeed give thanks well, but the other is not edified.

14:18 I thank my God I speak with tongues more than you all;

14:19 yet in the church I would rather speak five words with my understanding, that I may teach others also, than ten thousand words in a tongue.

In this paragraph Paul explained that interpretation was necessary if a tongue was spoken in the assembly. The context indicates that he was referring to real languages, not to some kind of ecstatic utterance (note especially 14:10-11). He drew illustrations from inanimate objects as well, for the sound of musical instruments must be meaningful and the sound of the battle trumpet must be certain. The act of speaking in tongues in the gathering of the church was to be for a purpose, as it was on the day of Pentecost when the Jews from fifteen different nations heard the Galilean disciples speaking in all the native languages of those present. There is nothing edifying about unintelligible sounds, and above all things those who speak in the church should edify those present. In other words, the gift of tongues was to serve the practical purpose of imparting information in a language that would mean something to someone in the congregation.

There was a certain emotional uplift apparently for the one speaking in a tongue, but this was of no lasting value to the speaker and did not impart any real spiritual growth to the hearer, since he could only hear the sounds, but could not understand what was being said.

Paul therefore resolved that he would be silent if no one present could interpret the language he was speaking. One who could understand a speaker and who would be moved to express agreement would make that known by saying "Amen" (14:16), but how could he say "Amen" meaningfully to something he did not understand at all?

As a chosen apostle Paul obviously was given an abundance of the sign gifts. He expressed this in regard to tongues (14:18), but had no desire merely to exhibit his gift. What he sought was the upbuilding of the church. The contrast between five words spoken with understanding and ten thousand words in another language which would not be understood is striking. It perhaps becomes even more so when we remember that "ten thousand" was the largest numeral in the Greek system of numbering (anything beyond that would be multiples of ten thousand). Later in this same chapter he spelled out the standards for speaking in tongues in the church.

In the light of this passage it is difficult to see how one could insist on the gift of tongues as a sign of the baptism of the Holy Spirit. There does not seem to be in scripture any equivalence between the gift of tongues and a spiritual life (see above in 3:1-4).

TONGUES AS A SIGN (14:20-25)

14:20 Brethren, do not be children in understanding; however, in malice be babes, but in understanding be mature.

14:21 In the law it is written:
"With men of other tongues and other lips
I will speak to this people;
And yet, for all that, they will not hear Me,"
says the Lord.

14:22 Therefore tongues are for a sign, not to those who

14:22 believe but to unbelievers; but prophesying is not
for unbelievers but for those who believe.

14:23 Therefore if the whole church comes together in
one place, and all speak with tongues, and there
come in those who are uninformed or unbelievers,
will they not say that you are out of your mind?

14:24 But if all prophesy, and an unbeliever or an uninformed person comes in, he is convinced by all, he
is convicted by all.

14:25 And thus the secrets of his heart are revealed; and
so, falling down on his face, he will worship God
and report that God is truly among you.

At first glance there seems to be a contradiction in what Paul said
about the purpose of tongues. He stated that tongues were a sign
for unbelievers, yet he also said that an unbeliever hearing the
tongues-speaking would think those speaking to be out of their
mind. How, then, could this be a sign?

The distinction is between the gift of tongues as intended, and
as manifested at Pentecost, and the misuse or abuse of the gift
by the Corinthians. They were using the gift not for edification
but for self-glorification. With a scene of disorder, with chaotic
and seemingly meaningless noise, they were repelling unbelievers, not attracting them.

Prophesying, on the other hand, could impart an intelligible
and edifying message, which the Holy Spirit could use to bring
conviction to the heart of unsaved people attending the services.
It would also build up the believers who would profit immeasur-
ably from a "Thus the Lord says." We have the inspired word of
God in writing, "the . . . Holy Scriptures, which are able to make
you wise for salvation through faith which is in Christ Jesus" (2
Timothy 3:15).

MAINTAINING ORDER IN THE MEETINGS OF THE CHURCH (14:26-40)

14:26 How is it then, brethren? Whenever you come
together, each of you has a psalm, has a teaching,
has a tongue, has a revelation, has an interpretation. Let all things be done for edification.

14:27 If anyone speaks in a tongue, let there be two or at
the most three, each in turn, and let one interpret.

14:28 But if there is no interpreter, let him keep silent in church, and let him speak to himself and to God.

14:29 Let two or three prophets speak, and let the others judge.

14:30 But if anything is revealed to another who sits by, let the first keep silent.

14:31 For you can all prophesy one by one, that all may learn and all may be encouraged.

14:32 And the spirits of the prophets are subject to the prophets.

14:33 For God is not the author of confusion but of peace, as in all the churches of the saints.

14:34 Let your women keep silent in the churches, for they are not permitted to speak; but they are to be submissive, as the law also says.

14:35 And if they want to learn something, let them ask their own husbands at home; for it is shameful for women to speak in church.

14:36 Or did the word of God come originally from you? Or was it you only that it reached?

14:37 If anyone thinks himself to be a prophet or spiritual, let him acknowledge that the things which I write to you are the comandments of the Lord.

14:38 But if anyone is ignorant, let him be ignorant.

14:39 Therefore, brethren, desire earnestly to prophesy, and do not forbid to speak with tongues.

14:40 Let all things be done decently and in order.

The instructions Paul gave about the conduct of church meetings show that there were liberty and informality in the services. Obviously the early believers had no elaborate church buildings and no formalism and ritualism such as developed eventually. The worship was conducted with wide participation, in many respects like a testimony and prayer meeting as in the midweek services of many evangelical churches today, except that in the first-century church there were still the sign gifts as God's manifestation of approval (Hebrews 2:1-3).

The general principle that Paul enunciated is orderliness (note the summation in 14:40). Whatever is done and said has to have the purpose of building up the believers ("Let all things be done for edification" [14:26]).

Speaking in tongues was not to monopolize the service, because no more than three persons were to exercise this gift in one meeting, preferably one or two, and never more than one at a time ("each in turn" [14:27]). Furthermore this gift was never to be manifested unless someone was present who had the gift of interpretation (14:28). God does not want his people to indulge in meaningless sounds, either as speakers or as listeners. These simple principles alone, if followed today, would eliminate practically all that passes for speaking in tongues.

Even in the exercise of the gift of prophecy there were to be sobriety and decorum, which would prohibit the frenzied speech and behavior accompanying "prophecy" in the pagan religions. Verse 32 is of special importance, for in the mystery religions and cults the so-called prophets and prophetesses worked themselves into a complete lack of self-control. "And the spirits of the prophets are subject to the prophets." This is in harmony with many other scriptures, which clearly teach that the "fruit of the Spirit is . . . self-control" (Galatians 5:23). Those who are under God's sovereign control are the most self-controlled of all people. The utterances of the prophets, therefore, were sober and orderly, while at the same time they were emphatic and self-assured.

In addition to the other commands there is the one concerning women's participation or non-participation. This should be compared with chapter 11 (*supra*) and with 1 Timothy 2:11-15. The present reference (14:34) appears to be related to other possible disorders. It may be that women were keeping up a conversation which was disturbing to others. Verse 35 seems to bear this out.

In this context the command would certainly include speaking in tongues, whatever else may be included. It may be significant that many women are deeply involved in the modern "charismatic movement," and have assumed a leading role in it.

If these instructions were obeyed literally and exactly, this movement would probably collapse. The true prophet in Paul's day and the one who was truly spiritual would willingly acknowledge that Paul's words were indeed "the commandments of the Lord" (14:37). Paul expressed himself ready, however, to disregard the obstinate and self-opinionated. Such a person may be left in his ignorance (but see NIV, which reads, "If he ignores this, he himself will be ignored," following the Aland-United Bible Society text).

SUBJECT FIVE
Resurrection
1 Corinthians 15

15:1 Moreover, brethren, I declare to you the gospel which I preached to you, which also you received and in which you stand,

15:2 by which also you are saved, if you hold fast that word which I preached to you—unless you believed in vain.

15:3 For I delivered to you first of all that which I also received: that Christ died for our sins according to the Scriptures,

15:4 and that He was buried, and that He rose again the third day according to the Scriptures,

15:5 and that He was seen by Cephas, then by the twelve.

15:6 After that He was seen by over five hundred brethren at once, of whom the greater part remain to the present, but some have fallen asleep.

15:7 After that He was seen by James, then by all the apostles.

15:8 Then last of all He was seen by me also, as by one born out of due time.

15:9 For I am the least of the apostles, who am not worthy to be called an apostle, because I persecuted the church of God.

15:10 But by the grace of God I am what I am, and His grace toward me was not in vain; but I labored more abundantly than they all, yet not I, but the grace of God which was with me.

15:11 Therefore, whether it was I or they, so we preach
and so you believed.

We have seen that 1 Corinthians does not deal with doctrine primarily. This chapter is an exception. Among the difficult questions that the Corinthians asked Paul in their letter was this one
on the resurrection. Although the familiar expression "now concerning" is not used, the location of the chapter seems to imply
that this was one of the questions. There were some in Corinth
who denied a bodily resurrection for believers (15:12). Apparently
they were not deliberately denying Christ's resurrection, but
seemed not to see the implications of their teaching.

Paul began this topic by reminding them of the content of the
gospel, the "good news" (cf. Romans 1:1-2). He again emphasized
the sequence of historical events: "I preached . . . you received
. . . you stand . . . you are saved."

Those who did not hold fast would thereby give evidence that
they had not been saved in the first place (cf. 1 John 2:19). Paul
knew, of course, that those who had truly believed had not
"believed in vain" (15:2).

This mention of the gospel is reminiscent of Paul's earlier statement of his preaching when he first came to Corinth: "Jesus Christ
and Him crucified" (2:2). Many have pointed out that the various
world religions are based on what teachers and leaders have *said*.
In contrast, the Christian faith is based primarily on what the Lord
Jesus Christ *did*. This is not to minimize his teaching.

That "Christ died" is a fact of history; that he "died for our
sins" is a statement of theology based on that historical event.
His burial and his resurrection are also true historical events, so
that our faith rests on a solid foundation of who Christ is and
what he has done.

"First of all" probably means "of first importance"; again we are
reminded of 2:2. In his message on himself as the "good shepherd" (John 10), the Lord Jesus spoke of the voluntary character
of his death, and said, "No one takes it [My life] from Me, but I lay
it down of Myself. I have power to lay it down and I have power
to take it again" (John 10:18). The fact that he took it again in resurrection is the evidence that all he had said was true. If his body
had remained in the grave, there would have been no evidence
for the truth of his amazing claims. The resurrection, as has often
been said, is the chief evidential fact of the Christian faith.

Like every other historical event, the resurrection is manifested by the testimony of witnesses. This is not a complete list of the appearances during the forty days between his resurrection and ascension, but the majority of them. The variety of his appearances in time and to different individuals and groups is conclusive to anyone willing to submit to the evidence.

Although Paul did not attempt to combat false theories about Christ's resurrection, the positive presentation of the facts clears away the false views. For example, the religious leaders in Jerusalem would have gone to any length to stop the disciples' preaching about the resurrection. The most logical way would have been to produce the body of Jesus, but they could not do that. The oldest attempt to explain away the resurrection was the theory that the disciples had stolen the body. This was the false account the members of the tomb guard gave after being bribed by the religious leaders (Matthew 28:11-15).

Another popular view among deniers of the resurrection is that the disciples suffered from hallucinations. Wanting so much for him to rise from the dead, they finally convinced themselves that he had. It would be an interesting hallucination held by more than five hundred people, many of whom were still alive and still confident of the Lord's resurrection after a quarter of a century.

This theory, of course, does not take into account that the disciples had not believed or understood the Lord Jesus when he said he would rise from the dead (Luke 18:34). They were emphatically not eager to believe he had risen. Thomas, who was absent on one occasion when Christ appeared, was probably not different from the others in his skepticism. The attitude of the apostles is expressed in Mark 16:11,13-14.

"He was seen by Cephas" (15:5). Probably this private meeting with Peter gave that apostle opportunity to confess his sin of denial and to accept the Lord's forgiveness.

"Then by the twelve." This term is simply another way of saying "the apostles," even though there were literally only eleven remaining after the suicide of Judas Iscariot, and on one occasion—possibly the one mentioned here—Thomas was absent, so that there were only ten apostles present.

It is believed that the appearance to more than five hundred believers at once was on the mountain in Galilee where he had appointed the believers to meet him (Matthew 28:16-20).

The James who is mentioned (15:7) is undoubtedly "James the Lord's brother" (Galatians 1:19), who was not one of the twelve apostles and who had not been a believer during the Lord's earthly ministry (John 7:5). He had a prominent place later among the believers in Jerusalem and became the writer of the epistle of James.

Christ's appearance to Paul contains a number of unusual features. Paul's adversaries denied his true apostleship, usually on the ground that he had not been called and commissioned personally by the Lord Jesus. In the introduction to Galatians Paul went to some lengths to refute the false teachers and to show his apostleship. He insisted that he had seen Christ on the Damascus road—not a subjective vision, but a truly objective appearance (cf. Galatians 1:11-12). "As by one born out of due time." This expression, found only here in the New Testament means literally "an untimely birth."

Paul was thinking of himself as being like Israel, which will turn to Christ when he appears in glory at his second coming and will be saved (Zechariah 12:10-14). Paul, therefore, is a sort of foreview of that coming national salvation of Israel, since the glorified Lord Jesus appeared personally to him on the road to Damascus, just as he will appear to Israel in that future day (Zechariah 12:10; Romans 11:25-27; Revelation 1:7).

In his statement in 15:9 the apostle was not engaging in false modesty or seeking reassurance from anyone, but uttering the sober truth about himself. Although he did not continually talk about the life he lived before becoming a Christian, he never forgot and deeply regretted his murderous persecution of believers in Christ before he met the glorified savior.

"But by the grace of God I am what I am." Anything good in any of us comes by his free gift. That grace, which is further described in 2 Corinthians 12:9-10, not only provides salvation, but also supplies the power for daily living and service for Christ. Paul brought this paragraph to a close by reminding them again of his preaching and their acceptance of Christ, "so you believed." He reiterated and established the fact of Christ's bodily resurrection; he then proceeded to prove the resurrection of believers from the fact of Christ's resurrection.

CHRIST'S RESURRECTION THE GUARANTEE OF OURS (15:12-19)

> 15:12 Now if Christ is preached that He has been raised from the dead, how do some among you say that there is no resurrection of the dead?

15:13 But if there is no resurrection of the dead, then Christ is not risen.

15:14 And if Christ is not risen, then our preaching is empty and your faith is also empty.

15:15 Yes, and we are found false witnesses of God, because we have testified of God that He raised up Christ, whom He did not raise up—if in fact the dead do not rise.

15:16 For if the dead do not rise, then Christ is not risen.

15:17 And if Christ is not risen, your faith is futile; you are still in your sins!

15:18 Then also those who have fallen asleep in Christ have perished.

15:19 If in this life only we have hope in Christ, we are of all men the most pitiable.

Having reminded the Corinthians of the great truths of the gospel, including Christ's bodily resurrection from the dead, the apostle then proceeded to demonstrate how the Lord's resurrection guarantees our resurrection. The sentences that follow set forth ironclad logic.

First, he inquired of the false teachers: How can you say there is no bodily resurrection, when the Lord Jesus Christ has already risen? His resurrection has been established in the preceding paragraph. But, he continued, if you are right in saying there is no such thing as bodily resurrection, then Christ could not have risen either. And if Christ did not rise, then everything we have preached and you have previously accepted is false, and our whole life is based on that monstrous lie! What's the use of our preaching? It's all false. And in what did you repose your faith? It is falsely based and therefore meaningless.

Not only that, Paul continued, but we (that is, the apostles and other messengers of the gospel) are indicted as false witnesses. We have been propagating the worst kind of falsehood, because we have been telling unsuspecting dupes a most vicious lie. If there is no such thing as resurrection, then obviously God did not raise up Christ. We have compromised his holy name as well as our own testimony. Paul repeated and reemphasized that if the dead do not rise, then Christ, who clearly was dead, did not rise. And if he did not rise, then our faith is the most fragile, futile will-o'-the-wisp. You're not saved at all, he insisted, if there is no resurrection of the body. You still bear the load of your sins— not only that, but there is no hope for those believers who have died ("fallen asleep in Christ").

The response of the Athenians to Paul's message in Acts 17 was typical of unsaved Greeks. "When they heard of the resurrection of the dead, some mocked" (Acts 17:32). The Greek religions, like most religions, taught some kind of spirit existence after death, but the bodily resurrection was a new concept, an idea not readily accepted. Apparently some among the professed believers in Corinth had not shaken off their old pagan ideas.

The intensity with which Paul argued the reality of the bodily resurrection of Christ and of believers is compatible with scripture teaching that the resurrection is an integral and necessary part of the gospel. In 15:19 he voiced the despair that we all would have apart from the reality of the resurrection. The hope we have in Christ in this life is a grand one, but it is unfulfilled here and now. It awaits the future "adoption" (the son position) which will come when Christ returns (note Romans 8:15-23).

If Christ did not rise, then there is no such thing as resurrection, and then what hope do we have? Would we flit around forever as disembodied spirits in some dark and gloomy "underworld"? That was the Greek expectation. Have we given up the emoluments and comforts of this life for that? No wonder Paul called us "most pitiable" if that were the fact.

But it isn't the fact, as the next paragraph joyfully asserts.

THE ORDER IN RESURRECTION (15:20-28)

15:20 But now Christ is risen from the dead, and has become the firstfruits of those who have fallen asleep.

15:21 For since by man came death, by Man also came the resurrection of the dead.

15:22 For as in Adam all die, even so in Christ all shall be made alive.

15:23 But each one in his own order: Christ the firstfruits, afterward those who are Christ's at His coming.

15:24 Then comes the end, when He delivers the kingdom to God the Father, when He puts an end to all rule and all authority and power.

15:25   For He must reign till He has put all enemies under His feet.

15:26   The last enemy that will be destroyed is death.

15:27   For "He has put all things under His feet." But when He says, "all things are put under Him," it is evident that He who put all things under Him is excepted.

15:28   Now when all things are made subject to Him, then the Son Himself will also be subject to Him who put all things under Him, that God may be all in all.

It is wonderful to join in Paul's triumphant conclusion: "But now Christ is risen from the dead"! Some in our day try to explain the resurrection away. Without meaning to, they go back to the "gloomy-shade" idea of so many human religions, or at best the pagan Greek "Elysian fields." Apart from Christ and the holy scriptures there is nothing to look forward to. We can look forward to *our* resurrection because we can look back on *his* resurrection. He "has become the firstfruits of those who have fallen asleep."

In this paragraph Paul contrasted the old creation and the new, each with its respective head. "For since by man came death . . ." The historical account of this, of course, is in Genesis 3. The present passage is parallel to another theological passage in Romans 5:12-21. In Adam all die; that is, since Adam was the head of the race his sin affected all his descendants. One of the results of that sin, as God had forewarned him, was death—both spiritual and physical.

The Lord Jesus, in John 5, spoke of two resurrections: the resurrection of life and the resurrection of condemnation. Revelation 20 speaks of the "first resurrection," clearly the same as the "resurrection of life" mentioned by our Lord. We see in the current passage that this first resurrection, the resurrection of life, is in sections. The Lord Jesus Christ is first of all, here called the "firstfruits," just as the feast of the firstfruits in Israel, on the first day of the week during the week of Passover and unleavened bread, gave the promise of the coming spring harvest.

"Afterward those who are Christ's at His coming." This numerous contingent includes all the saved of the present church age, those to be "caught up" at the rapture (1 Thessalonians 4:17). There is difference of opinion whether the Old Testament saints are to be in this group or to be a part of the next company, "the end"; that is, the end of that particular resurrection. Some have used the terminology of firstfruits, harvest, and gleanings. This "end" company obviously will include the saved dead of the tribulation period. According to this key passage, everyone who will have been resurrected up to and including the time of the glorious return of the Lord Jesus Christ to establish his kingdom after the end of the tribulation (Daniel's seventieth week) is included in the "first resurrection," i.e., the "resurrection of life" (John 5:28-29). The rest of the dead will not be raised until after the millennium. That is the "resurrection of condemnation." All in that resurrection are lost (see Revelation 20:5,12). The order of events is: the rapture, followed in the heavenly spheres by the judgment of believers' works at the judgment seat of Christ and followed on the earth by the seven-year tribulation period; the coming of Christ in glory, followed by the judgment of living Israel (Ezekiel 20:33-38; Matthew 25:1-30) and of living gentiles (Matthew 25:31- 46); the resurrection of saints who have died during the tribulation period; the millennial kingdom; the judgment of the resurrected unsaved before the great white throne.

The present passage speaks of Christ's millennial reign, so often prophesied in the Old Testament, the "restoration of God's created order" (J.A. Martin), as foretold in Isaiah, the subject of a number of messianic and millennial psalms (cf. especially Psalm 8 and Psalm 110). For the historical background of putting "enemies under His feet," see Joshua 10:24.

As the agent of the godhead in restoring the rule of God to the earth, the Lord Jesus Christ is to reign with invincible power (e.g., Psalm 2:9). Every enemy will be put down and the last will be death itself, which entered into the world through Adam's sin. The way to destroy death is to raise everyone from the dead, as the millennial passage indicates.

Verses 27 and 28 are among the most difficult in this passage. Apparently Christ's mediatorial rule will be merged after the millennium with God's eternal sovereign rule of all things (cf. Psalm103:19). Then the grand eternal plan of redemption will have been brought to fruition, "that God may be all in all."

THE ERROR OF DENYING THE RESURRECTION (15:29-34)

> 15:29 Otherwise, what will they do who are baptized for the dead, if the dead do not rise at all? Why then are they baptized for the dead?

15:30 And why do we stand in jeopardy every hour?

15:31 I affirm, by the boasting in you which I have in Christ Jesus our Lord, I die daily.

15:32 If, in the manner of men, I have fought with beasts at Ephesus, what advantage is it to me? If the dead do not rise, "Let us eat and drink, for tomorrow we die."

15:33 Do not be deceived: "Evil company corrupts good habits."

15:34 Awake to righteousness, and do not sin; for some do not have the knowledge of God. I speak this to your shame.

Scores of interpretations have been suggested for 15:29. Here, as so often, it is easier to say what it does not mean than to explain what it does mean. Commentators claim to have seen innumerable interpretations, but of course many of them are similar. The analogy of scripture ought to make it clear to us that the statement does not mean that one can take someone else's place in baptism and transfer the merit of that act. No one's faith can be transferred in this way, much less the ordinance of water baptism, which in itself has no saving efficacy but is an outward sign of the baptism of the Holy Spirit within.

The Greek preposition *hyper* usually means "on behalf of," but it sometimes seems to be equivalent to *anti*. That appears to fit best here. New Christians are being baptized in the place of those who have been taken in death, thus filling up the ranks of the great company of believers. This fits in with the statement of the Lord Jesus when he said, "On this rock I will build My church, and the gates of Hades shall not prevail against it" (Matthew 16:18).

It would be a meaningless thing for people to go on following one another in this way if the whole process were actually based on misunderstanding and error. And what would be the use of jeopardizing one's life to help perpetuate an immense fraud? Paul was willing to be subject to constant danger of death ("I die daily") because he knew that his life was not meaningless, that the glory lay ahead, and that the resurrection would crown it all.

Paul's fighting with beasts at Ephesus (the place in which he was writing this epistle) probably is a reference not to literal beasts in an arena, but to the murderous opposition of bestial men. This cannot be a reference to the Ephesian riot in Acts 19, for Paul left Ephesus soon after that, and it would not harmonize with 16:8. The very early *Acts of Paul and Thecla*, one of the so-called New Testament apocryphal books, seems to be based on a mistaken interpretation of this statement. In this fanciful story Paul was quoted as saying to a lion that he met on the road, "Aren't you the lion that I baptized in the arena when you miraculously spared my life?" Whatever the passage means, it does not mean that!

The point the apostle made is that the truth of the resurrection makes the Christian life worthwhile, even if life includes all kinds of hardships and perils. If there were no resurrection, then the Epicureans and other hedonists might have a point. Of course they do not.

WHAT KIND OF BODY? (15:35-50)

15:35 But someone will say, "How are the dead raised up? And with what body do they come?"

15:36 Foolish one, what you sow is not made alive unless it dies.

15:37 And what you sow, you do not sow that body that shall be, but mere grain—perhaps wheat or some other grain.

15:38 But God gives it a body as He pleases, and to each seed its own body.

15:39 All flesh is not the same flesh, but there is one kind of flesh of men, another flesh of animals, another of fish, and another of birds.

15:40 There are also celestial bodies and terrestrial bodies; but the glory of the celestial is one, and the glory of the terrestrial is another.

15:41 There is one glory of the sun, another glory of the moon, and another glory of the stars; for one star differs from another star in glory.

15:42 So also is the resurrection of the dead. The body is sown in corruption, it is raised in incorruption.

15:43 It is sown in dishonor, it is raised in glory. It is sown in weakness, it is raised in power.

15:44 It is sown a natural body, it is raised a spiritual body. There is a natural body, and there is a spiritual body.

15:45 And so it is written, "The first man Adam became

a living being." The last Adam became a life-giving spirit.

15:46 However, the spiritual is not first, but the natural, and afterward the spiritual.

15:47 The first man was of the earth, made of dust; the second Man is the Lord from heaven.

15:48 As was the man of dust, so also are those who are made of dust; and as is the heavenly Man, so also are those who are heavenly.

15:49 And as we have borne the image of the man of dust, we shall also bear the image of the heavenly Man.

15:50 Now this I say, brethren, that flesh and blood cannot inherit the kingdom of God; nor does corruption inherit incorruption.

Having shown the necessity and the reality of the resurrection, the apostle next described the manner in which it will take place. The unbelieving scoffer will ask how this body can be reconstituted after it has decayed and dissolved. Paul used the analogy of planting seeds. In the late 1930s Dr. Irwin Moon of the Moody Institute of Science showed this process through time-lapse photography, further confirming the statement of the Lord Jesus (although his statements need no confirmation): "Most assuredly, I say to you, unless a grain of wheat falls into the ground and dies, it remains alone; but if it dies, it produces much grain" (John 12:24).

Scripture portrays God as he is involved in the germinating process ("as He pleases"). Verse 39 is a corroborating witness, along with many other scriptures, against the prevalent naturalism of Paul's own day and emphatically of ours. Genesis 1 repeatedly informs us that God has placed limits to the changing varieties of plants and animals he has created. Each reproduces "after [according to] its kind" (Genesis 1:11-12 [twice], 21 [twice], 24 [twice], 25 [three times]). "All flesh is not the same flesh" (15:39).

Continuing to use the analogy of the natural creation, the apostle reiterated God's sovereign pleasure in his creating of infinite variety in what he has made. In this day of electronic telescopes, we can be more aware than preceding generations of the limitless extent and the wonder of the universe, for we now see that "one star differs from another star in glory" (15:41). The God who made all these vast heavenly bodies certainly is able to recreate human bodies and to give them a glory far beyond our imagining. "So also is the resurrection of the dead" (15:42). The contrasts include imperishability as opposed to perishability, glory as opposed to dishonor, power as opposed to weakness; in short, a spiritual body as opposed to a soulish ("natural") body. The body as it is constituted in this life is adapted to the realm of the soul; the resurrection body will be adapted to the realm of the spirit, that within man which enables him to have fellowship with God. Although the terms *spirit* and *soul* are sometimes used interchangeably in scripture, there are some other passages that make a real distinction between them. Some examples are: 1 Thessalonians 5:23, "spirit and soul and body," where there seems to be as much distinction between the spirit and the soul as there is between the soul and the body; Hebrews 4:12, "the division of soul and spirit"; 1 Corinthians 2:14-15 (see *supra*), where the "natural" (soulish) man and the "spiritual" man are contrasted. The present passage seems to buttress the idea of trichotomy, as do the others just mentioned, as opposed to dichotomy (which, admittedly, is more widely held philosophically).

Note the contrast in 15:45: "The first man Adam became a living being [soul]." A more accurate translation of the next clause is, "The last Adam is a life-giving spirit." Note that there is no verb in this clause; consequently, the principle of Greek grammar is that the appropriate form of the verb *to be* should be supplied.

Adam's body, formed by God from elements in the soil previously created by him (such as carbon, hydrogen, oxygen, phosphorus, potassium, iodine, nitrogen, sulfur, calcium, iron, magnesium,manganese, sodium, chlorine, and traces of other elements), was perfectly adapted to this earthly environment before the entrance of sin into the world. We should never forget, however, that we are "of the earth earthy" (KJV). Yet our bearing the image of Christ is just as certain as our present state of bearing Adam's likeness. "Flesh and blood cannot inherit the kingdom of God" (cf. the words of the Lord Jesus to Nicodemus in John 3). There must be a radical change in our body to make our eternal heavenly dwelling possible (cf. also 2 Corinthians 5:1-2).

OUR CHANGED BODIES (15:51-58)

15:51   Behold, I tell you a mystery: We shall not all sleep, but we shall all be changed—

15:52   in a moment, in the twinkling of an eye, at the last trumpet. For the trumpet will sound, and the dead will be raised incorruptible, and we shall be changed.

15:53   For this corruptible must put on incorruption, and this mortal must put on immortality.

15:54   So when this corruptible has put on incorruption, and this mortal has put on immortality, then shall be brought to pass the saying that is written: "Death is swallowed up in victory."

15:55   "O death, where is your sting?
      O Hades, where is your victory?"

15:56   The sting of death is sin, and the strength of sin is the law.

15:57   But thanks be to God, who gives us the victory through our Lord Jesus Christ.

15:58   Therefore, my beloved brethren, be steadfast, immovable, always abounding in the work of the Lord, knowing that your labor is not in vain in the Lord.

Along with 1 Thessalonians 4:13-18 this is a key passage on the doctrine of the rapture. Many allege that the apostle Paul was absolutely certain that he would not die, but would live until the Lord's promised return (John 14:3). Therefore, the argument goes, since Paul was mistaken about this, he was probably mistaken about other things as well.

The premise is inaccurate; there is no passage in which Paul stated unequivocally that he would remain until the Lord returned. He did express his wish that this might be so. His attitude was that which all Christians should exhibit: to be expecting the Lord at any moment. This passage and 1 Thessalonians 4 speak of the Lord's return from the viewpoint of those who will be alive at that great event. After all, whenever the Lord comes back, there will be a whole generation of believers who will not die, but will be changed and caught up in an instant. Since that is the case, what more proper and accurate form of expression could be used than the first person plural "we" (that is, believers still alive at that time)? That Paul was aware he might not live until the Lord's return is demonstrated in 2 Corinthians 5:1-9, which manifests just as sublime faith among those Christians who will die before the Lord's return. The "we know" in 2 Corinthians 5:1 no more indicates certainty of dying before the rapture than the other passages demonstrate certainty of living until the rapture. Our Lord has shown emphatically that date-setting for his return is wrong (Matthew 25:13; Mark 13:32; Luke 12:40,46). No one can state dogmatically that the Lord Jesus is coming back at a particular time. What every Christian should say is that the Lord Jesus may come back at any moment; therefore all believers should be living in readiness for his appearing (cf. 1 Thessalonians 1:8-10; Philippians 3:20-21).

We must distinguish carefully between the rapture (from the description of the event in the words "caught up" in 1 Thessalonians 4:17), which is the coming of the Lord Jesus Christ for his own as he promised in John 14:3, and the second coming of Christ in glory to set up his millennial kingdom as foretold in many prophetic passages in both Testaments. The rapture is specifically called here "a mystery" (the Greek word means literally "a secret"). This truth, as distinguished from the glorious coming of Christ to reign, was not clearly revealed in the Old Testament. Comparison of the passages in the New Testament which contain the word *musterion* will bear out this explanation of its technical meaning. Recall the words by Edward Bickersteth: "Some from earth, from glory some, / Severed only 'Till He come!'"

The change is to be instantaneous. The Greek word translated "moment" is *atomos*, from which is derived the English word *atom*, meaning originally, "that which is indivisible." The "twinkling of an eye" is not the blinking of the eyelid but the reflection of light by the eye.

In the marching orders for Israel, as described in Numbers 10, the trumpeters sounded an advance and the tribes set forward. This heavenly trumpet is the immediate signal to "meet the Lord in the air" (1 Thessalonians 4:17).

Those believers who have died will rise in new bodies "conformed to His glorious body" (Philippians 3:21). These bodies retain their identity, but oh! how different in quality. The living saints will then immediately be changed in the same way, and all will be "caught up . . . to meet the Lord in the air" (1 Thessalonians 4:17).

The conclusion of this section in 15:58 reminds us again of the practical nature of this letter. Doctrine is vital, and basic to all knowledge and conduct, but it is not presented in scripture in order to puff up believers with their superior knowledge. It gives the motive and the dynamic for correct action. Repeatedly in scripture we are reminded of the goal toward which we press (cf. Philippians 3:12-14).

SUBJECT SIX
The Collection and Other Matters
1 Corinthians 16:1-11

PRINCIPLES OF CHRISTIAN STEWARDSHIP (16:1-4)

16:1 Now concerning the collection for the saints, as I have given orders to the churches of Galatia, so you must do also:

16:2 On the first day of the week let each one of you lay something aside, storing up as he may prosper, that there be no collections when I come.

16:3 And when I come, whomever you approve by your letters, I will send to bear your gift to Jerusalem.

16:4 But if it is fitting that I go also, they will go with me.

Some people believe that money should never be discussed in the church. Paul considered it entirely proper to mention money; in fact, it is correct to say that the Holy Spirit considered it right to do so. We have already noted in chapter 9 that Paul refused to take money from the Corinthian church, but this was a special case.

Some may consider this anticlimactic. The apostle had just described the glories of the resurrection body and the mystery of the rapture and reminded those to whom the letter was addressed that they had every reason to continue energetically and wholeheartedly in the work of the Lord. In the next breath, so to speak, he dictated to his secretary, "Now concerning the collection for the saints."

No, this is not an anticlimax, nor is it out of place. Paul was broaching here a subject that had lain heavily on his heart. Even though he was "an apostle to the Gentiles" (Romans 11:13), he always was searching for ways in which to win to Christ some from among his kindred, the Jews. Also, because of his realization of what blessing had come to gentile believers through Jewish believers, he wanted to encourage this mutual assistance. In his letter to the Romans, probably written after 1 Corinthians, he explained the rationale of the "collection for the saints":

> But now I am going to Jerusalem to minister to the saints. For it pleased those from Macedonia and Achaia to make a certain contribution for the poor among the saints who are in Jerusalem. It pleased them indeed, and they are their debtors. For if the Gentiles have been partakers of their spiritual things, their duty is also to minister to them in material things (Romans 15:25-27).

In his second letter to the Corinthians (chapters 8–9) Paul gave more detailed instructions concerning this project as an outstanding example of Christian stewardship. Here he was content merely to emphasize the importance of systematic ("on the first day of the week") and proportionate ("as he may prosper") giving. One who reads the fuller passage in 2 Corinthians will be impressed with the orderly and careful way funds were handled.

THE APOSTLE'S PLANS (16:5-11)

16:5 Now I will come to you when I pass through Macedonia (for I am passing through Macedonia).

16:6 And it may be that I will remain, or even spend the winter with you, that you may send me on my journey, wherever I go.

16:7 For I do not wish to see you now on the way; but I hope to stay a while with you, if the Lord permits.

16:8 But I will tarry in Ephesus until Pentecost.

16:9 For a great and effective door has opened to me, and there are many adversaries.

16:10 And if Timothy comes, see that he may be with you without fear; for he does the work of the Lord, as I also do.

16:11 Therefore let no one despise him. But send him on

his journey in peace, that he may come to me; for
I am waiting for him with the brethren.

The close relationship between the apostle Paul and his converts
is often seen in this epistle in spite of the difficulties and misun-
derstandings. There is again in 16:7 an intimation of his reluc-
tance to return to Corinth until the major difficulties had been
settled (cf. 4:21). It is not that he did not want to see them, but
that he wanted to see them under favorable conditions and with
the opportunity of making an extended visit, not a hurried and
brief stay (16:7).

Verse 8 is our clue for saying that Paul wrote and sent this letter from Ephesus. Probably his plans to stay there until Pentecost (late May or early June, fifty days after the feast of first
fruits, called in the Old Testament the feast of weeks) were dis-
rupted by the riot described in Acts 19.

We can understand something of the dedication of the apostle
when we see that the presence of "many adversaries" would not
deter him from entering that "great and effective door."

Paul obviously had a tender regard for his young fellow servant, Timothy, who had joined him on his second missionary
journey and who ministered untiringly to Paul and other members of the missionary group. Some might have a tendency to
look down on him (16:11; cf. 1 Timothy 4:12) because of his com-
parative youth and inexperience, but Paul recognized his value.

SUBJECT SEVEN
Concerning Apollos and Closing Greetings
1 Corinthians 16:12-24

> 16:12 Now concerning our brother Apollos, I strongly urged him to come to you with the brethren, but he was quite unwilling to come at this time; however, he will come when he has a convenient time.

Even though little is told about Apollos, it seems proper to regard this verse as a subject by itself. The use of the familiar "now concerning" informs us that the Corinthians had asked about Apollos in their letter. Like Paul and Peter, Apollos was a victim, not a culprit, in the factional troubles and outbreaks of strife and the quarreling over human leaders.

We can conjecture that the divisions in the church may have been the main reason that Apollos did not want to visit Corinth at this time. Paul's statement about Apollos's unwillingness to come gives insight also into the relationships of apostles and their coworkers in the early church. Paul obviously had no authority to command or compel Apollos to visit Corinth. The Holy Spirit sovereignly directed his workers and each was accountable to him.

Apollos is mentioned by name only ten times in the New Testament, seven of those times in this epistle (Acts 18:24; 19:1; 1 Corinthians 1:12; 3:4,5,6,22; 4:6; 16:12; Titus 3:13). Yet we feel that we know him and can love him as a brother in Christ. Luke's characterization of him as "an eloquent man and mighty in the

Scriptures" (Acts 18:24) has endeared him to all succeeding generations of believers.

CLOSING EXHORTATIONS AND GREETINGS (16:13-24)

16:13 Watch, stand fast in the faith, be brave, be strong.
16:14 Let all that you do be done with love.
16:15 I urge you, brethren—you know the household of Stephanas, that it is the firstfruits of Achaia, and that they have devoted themselves to the ministry of the saints—
16:16 that you also submit to such, and to everyone who works and labors with us.
16:17 I am glad about the coming of Stephanas, Fortunatus, and Achaicus, for what was lacking on your part they supplied.
16:18 For they refreshed my spirit and yours. Therefore acknowledge such men.
16:19 The churches of Asia greet you. Aquila and Priscilla greet you heartily in the Lord, with the church that is in their house.
16:20 All the brethren greet you. Greet one another with a holy kiss.
16:21 The salutation with my own hand—Paul's.
16:22 If anyone does not love the Lord Jesus Christ, let him be accursed. O Lord, come!
16:23 The grace of our Lord Jesus Christ be with you.
16:24 My love be with you all in Christ Jesus. Amen.

Paul's exhortations were not complaining or nagging. We can detect in his urgent pleas his heartbeat, and above all, the heartbeat of his Lord. The household of Stephanas, mentioned here (16:15), had been mentioned also in 1:16 as among those baptized by Paul, evidently early in his Corinthian ministry, for he called them here "the firstfruits of Achaia."

The coming of these friends to Paul at Ephesus helps us to realize the extent of travel in the apostolic age. The Roman roads and the peaceful condition of the Mediterranean, freed of pirates, made travel comparatively easy, much more so than in the middle ages and until fairly recent times, but nevertheless painfully slow by our present-day standards.

"Asia" (16:19) did not mean in Paul's day the vast continent of Asia, but a Roman province in the western area of what we call Asia Minor (in the modern country of Turkey). Ephesus, the city from which Paul was writing, is one of the cities listed in Revelation a generation later, near the close of the first century, as one of the "churches of Asia."

Paul had first met Aquila and Priscilla in Corinth (Acts 18:1-3), and in addition to sharing with him in the trade of tentmaking, they had been his loyal supporters and fellow workers in the gospel. Now some years later they were living in Ephesus and sent their greetings back to the church in Corinth. They probably had flourished in their business enough to have a sizable house, which they made available to a "church," a congregation of believers (16:19).

Verse 21 verifies that Paul's normal practice was to dictate his letters to a secretary, but personally to sign his name in order to demonstrate the genuineness of the message (cf. 2 Thessalonians 3:17).

Some readers of the KJV have been perplexed at 16:22, which in that translation retains the two foreign words, *anathema* and *maranatha*. The former word is Greek, and is translated in NKJV and others as "accursed." A similar thought is expressed in Galatians 1:8-9, where the same Greek word is used.

The other word is Aramaic and has the beautiful meaning, "Oh Lord come!" Final and utter rejection of Christ can lead only to eternal judgment. Paul was not happy that people are lost and on their way to hell, but he recognized that when the Lord comes, judgment will be sealed, and that only the personal coming of the Lord Jesus Christ can make things right. Therefore, while solemnly pronouncing the judgment of those who do not love the Lord Jesus (the ultimate sin), he nevertheless longed for the personal appearance of the Lord.

At the close of the letter, as at the beginning, Paul prayed for God's grace for them (16:23) and expressed his own personal love for them (16:24).

We know more about the church at Corinth than we do about any other church of the New Testament time. Our brief study, we trust, has enabled us to recognize the theme stated at the beginning: *the gospel in its personal, practical, and social implications.* The gospel is "the power of God to salvation for everyone who believes" (Romans 1:16), and that same gospel which saves us also instructs us in its application, which is as broad as the whole of life (cf. Titus 2:11-14). Paul has declared to the Corinthians and to us "the gospel," by which we have been saved and in which we stand (1Corinthians 15:1).

APPENDIX

NOTES ON APOSTOLIC CHRONOLOGY

E. J. Bickerman in *Chronology of the Ancient World* (Cornell University Press, 1969), lamented that "knowledge is required to prepare a work of scholarship, but only ignorance gives the courage to publish it" (page 7). This was *apropos* of the difficulties and uncertainties of ancient chronology.

In spite of the great amount of research given to New Testament chronology, there are few aspects that can be dated dogmatically. Some events can be dated from extrabiblical sources, such as the proconsulship of Gallio, which has been identified from an inscription at Delphi as occurring in A.D. 51 and 52.

If we accept the traditional date for Paul's arrival in Rome as a prisoner—the spring of A.D. 61—we can work back to his arrest in Jerusalem two years before and further back to his extended stay in Ephesus on his third missionary journey.

In spite of the immense amount of work done by Sir William M. Ramsay, the older system advocated in the nineteenth century by Bishop J.B. Lightfoot still has great appeal to the present writer. In his commentary on Galatians, Lightfoot has an essay on dates of Paul's life and epistles that has an inner consistency and does not controvert the few facts that are known.

Harold W. Hoehner's work, *Chronological Aspects of the Life of Christ*, while not bearing directly on the present subject, helps to chart a course that in the end shows the strength of many of the traditional views. Placing the beginning of our Lord's public ministry in the summer or autumn of A.D. 29 and declaring for a ministry of three and a half years, Hoehner insists on A.D. 33 as the year of the crucifixion and the resurrection.

Another event that helps in some measure to date Paul's life and ministry is the procuratorship of Felix. If Felix came to this office in A.D. 52, as seems most probable, Paul's statement in Acts

24:10 ("You have been for many years a judge of this nation") could hardly be reconciled with a date of 55 or 56 for his appearance before Felix, as Boyer intimates in his article, "Chronology of the New Testament," in the *Wycliffe Bible Encyclopedia*.

First Corinthians has been dated variously from A.D. 55 to 59. Lightfoot's observation that Paul's letters are in four groups separated by approximately five-year intervals has real merit. His conclusion that 1 Corinthians was written in the spring (16:8) of 57 seems to fit into a coherent system.

It seems very likely that Paul was released from his first Roman imprisonment (actually a form of "house arrest," see Acts 28:30-31) before the burning of Rome, which occurred in A.D. 64. Early tradition strongly supports this view, and this coincides with Paul's confidence in Philippians 1:19-26 and in Philemon 22 that he would be released.

As noted in the commentary, then, Paul's evangelistic ministry in Corinth can be dated in A.D. 51 and 52, and the writing of 1 Corinthians from Ephesus in the spring of 57. In view of his three-year stay in Ephesus on his third missionary journey, he could hardly have been arrested in Jerusalem before 59. The two years in Caesarea would be 59 and 60, with arrival in Rome as a prisoner in the spring of 61, release in the spring of 63, further travel throughout the empire, a second arrest, and martyrdom in 68. Paul was expecting this as he wrote his last letter, 2 Timothy (note especially 2 Timothy 4:6-8).

SELECT BIBLIOGRAPHY

(The listing of a work in this bibliography does not indicate either agreement or disagreement with it.)

COMMENTARIES ON 1 CORINTHIANS

Badcock, F.J. *The Pauline Epistles and the Epistle to the Hebrews in Their Historical Setting.* London: SPCK and New York: The Macmillan Company, 1937.

Barclay, William. *The Letters to the Corinthians.* Philadelphia: The Westminster Press, 2d ed., 1956. *Daily Study Bible.*

Barrett, C.K. *A Commentary on the First Epistle to the Corinthians.* New York and Evanston: Harper and Row, Publishers, 1968. *Harper's New Testament Commentaries.*

Beet, Joseph Agar. *A Commentary on St. Paul's Epistles to the Corinthians,* 6th ed. London: Hodder and Stoughton, 1895.

Bratcher, Robert G. *A Translator's Guide to Paul's First Letter to the Corinthians.* London, New York, Stuttgart: United Bible Societies, 1982.

Calvin, John. *The First Epistle of Paul the Apostle to the Corinthians* (John W. Fraser, translator). Grand Rapids: William B. Eerdmans Publishing Company, 1960.

Darby, John Nelson. *Notes of Readings on the Epistles to the Corinthians.* London: G. Morrish (n.d.).

Edwards, Thomas Charles. *A Commentary on the First Epistle to the Corinthians.* New York: A.C. Armstrong and Son, 1886.

Ellicott, Charles J. *St. Paul's First Epistle to the Corinthians.* London: Longmans, Green and Co., 1887.

Findlay, George G. *The Epistles of Paul the Apostle: A Sketch of Their Origin and Contents.* New York: Wilbur B. Ketcham (n.d.).

Godet, F. *Commentary on St. Paul's First Epistle to the Corinthians* (Two Volumes), A. Cusin, translator. Edinburgh: T. and T. Clark (n.d.). *Clark's Foreign Theological Library.*

Goudge, H.L. *The First Epistle to the Corinthians.* London: Methuen and Co., 1903. *Westminster Commentaries.*

Gromacki, Robert A. *Called to Be Saints: An Exposition of First Corinthians.* Grand Rapids: Baker, 1981.

Grosheide, F.W. *Commentary on the First Epistle to the Corinthians.* Grand Rapids: William B. Eerdmans Publishing Co., 1953. *New International Commentary.*

Ironside, H.A. *Addresses on the First Epistle to the Corinthians.* Neptune, New Jersey: Loizeaux Brothers, Inc., 1941.

Johnson, S. Lewis, Jr. "I Corinthians" in *The Wycliffe Bible Commentary* edited by Charles F. Pfeiffer and Everett F. Harrison. Chicago: Moody Press, 1962.

Kling, Christian Friedrich (Daniel W. Poor, translator). *The First Epistle of Paul to the Corinthians.* New York: Charles Scribner's Sons, 1915.

Lightfoot, J.B. *Notes on the Epistles of St. Paul.* Grand Rapids: Zondervan Publishing House, 1957. *Classic Commentary Library.*

Lowery, David K. "First Corinthians" in *The Bible Knowledge Commentary, New Testament* edited by John F. Walvoord and Roy B. Zuck. Wheaton, Illinois: Victor Books, 1983.

Luck, G. Coleman. *First Corinthians.* Chicago: Moody Press, 1958. *Everyman's Bible Commentary.*

MacArthur, John, Jr. *The MacArthur New Testament Commentary: 1 Corinthians.* Chicago: Moody Press, 1984.

McPheeters, Julian C. *The Epistles to the Corinthians.* Grand Rapids: Baker Book House, 1964. *Proclaiming the New Testament.*

Meyer, H.A.W. (D. Douglas Bannerman, translator). *Critical and Exegetical Hand-Book to the Epistles to the Corinthians.* New York: Funk and Wagnalls, 1884.

Morgan, G. Campbell. *The Corinthian Letters of Paul.* New York: Fleming H. Revell Company, 1946.

Murphy-O'Connor, Jerome. *First Corinthians (New Testament Message).* Wilmington, Delaware: Michael Glazier, Inc., 1979, 1982.

Redpath, Alan. *The Royal Route to Heaven—Studies in First Corinthians.* Westwood, New Jersey: Fleming H. Revell Co., 1960.

Robertson, Archibald, and Alfred Plummer. *A Critical and Exegetical Commentary on the First Epistle of St. Paul to the*

Corinthians. Edinburgh: T. and T. Clark, 2d ed., 1914 (1967 reprint). *International Critical Commentary.*

Robertson, Archibald Thomas. *Word Pictures in the New Testament*, Volume IV. New York and London: Harper and Brothers Publishers, 1931.

Robertson, Frederick W. *Expository Lectures on St. Paul's Epistles to the Corinthians.* London: Henry S. King and Co., 1872.

Shaw, R.D. *The Pauline Epistles: Introductory and Expository Studies*, 3d ed. Edinburgh: T. and T. Clark, 1909.

Vaughan, Curtis, and Thomas D. Lea. *First Corinthians (Bible Study Commentary).* Grand Rapids: Zondervan Publishing House, 1983.

Vine, W.E. *First Corinthians.* London and Edinburgh: Oliphants, Ltd., 1951.

Wiersbe, Warren W. *Be Wise.* Wheaton, Illinois: Victor Books, 1984.

GENERAL WORKS

Barrett, C.K. *Essays on Paul.* London: SPCK, 1982.

Bickerman, E.J. *Chronology of the Ancient World.* Ithaca, New York: Cornell University Press, 1969.

Brown, John. *The Resurrection of Life: an Exposition of First Corinthians XV.* London: William Oliphant, 1866 (1978 reprint by Klock and Klock Christian Publishers, Minneapolis).

Clemens Romanus. "Epistle to the Corinthians," in *The Ante-Nicene Fathers*, Volume I. Buffalo: The Christian Literature Publishing Co., 1886.

Conybeare, W.J., and J.S. Howson. *The Life and Epistles of the Apostle Paul.* New York: Thomas Y. Crowell & Co. (n.d.).

Dahl, M.E. *The Resurrection of the Body.* Naperville, Illinois: Alec R. Allenson, Inc., 1962.

Dale, James W. *An Inquiry into the Usage of BAPTIZO, and the Nature of Christic and Patristic Baptism.* Philadelphia: Presbyterian Board of Publication, 1874.

Gangel, Kenneth O. *The Gospel and the Gay.* Nashville: Thomas Nelson Publishers, 1978.

Gloag, Paton J. *Introduction to the Pauline Epistles.* Edinburgh: T. and T. Clark, 1874.

Grun, Bernard. *The Timetables of History.* New York: Simon and Schuster, 1982.

Hiebert, D. Edmond. *An Introduction to the Pauline Epistles.* Chicago: Moody Press, 1954.

Lightfoot, J.B. *The Epistle of St. Paul to the Galatians.* Grand Rapids: Zondervan Publishing House, 1978.

Martin, John R. *Divorce and Remarriage.* Herald Press, 1974.

Murphy-O'Connor, Jerome. *St. Paul's Corinth: Texts and Archaeology.* Wilmington, Delaware: Michael Glazier, Inc., 1983.

Murray, John. *Divorce.* Committee on Christian Education, Orthodox Presbyterian Church, 1953.

Papahatzis, Nicos. *Ancient Corinth.* Athens: Ekdotike Athenon, S. A., 1981.

Pfeiffer, Charles F., and Howard F. Vos. *Wycliffe Historical Geography of Bible Lands.* Chicago: Moody Press, 1967.

Plato (Benjamin Jowett, translator). *Symposium* (in *Great Books of the Western World*). Chicago: University of Chicago Press.

Purves, George T. *Christianity in the Apostolic Age.* New York: Charles Scribner's Sons, 1931.

Ramsay, Sir William M. *St. Paul the Traveller and the Roman Citizen* (New Edition). Grand Rapids: Baker Book House (1982 reprint of Hodder and Stoughton's 15th ed., 1925).

Smith, David. *The Life and Letters of St. Paul.* New York: George H. Doran Company (n.d.).

Smith, William. *Dictionary of Greek and Roman Geography* (2 vols.). Boston: Little, Brown, and Company, 1870.

Theissen, Gerd (John H. Schuetz, translator). *The Social Setting of Pauline Christianity.* Philadelphia: Fortress Press, 1982.

Williams, John. *For Every Cause?* Neptune, New Jersey: Loizeaux Brothers, Inc., 1981.

SCRIPTURE INDEX

GENESIS

1:11-12	138
1:21	138
1:24-25	138
2:24-25	138
3	134
4:19	71
6:8	22
11:1	119
19	13, 61
39:8-9, 12	64

EXODUS

3:1	32
15:20	101
17:1-7	94
32:6	95

LEVITICUS

4:2	34
18	70
20	70

NUMBERS

10	141
14:1-4	95
25:9	95

DEUTERONOMY

17:7	57
19:19	57
22:21-24	57
24:7	57

JOSHUA

10:24	135

JUDGES

4:4	101
19	13

2 SAMUEL

12:10-14	64
23:2	36

2 KINGS

22:14	101

NEHEMIAH

13	75

JOB

1:12	53
2:3	54
2:6	53

PSALMS

2:9	135
8	135
24:1	98
51:16	34
95	95
103:19	135
106:8-9	94
110	135
136:13-15	94

PROVERBS	30
5:15-20	71
20:1	103
23:31-35	103
ECCLESIASTES	43
1:2	43
ISAIAH	
35	110
40:13	38
JEREMIAH	
9:24	30
EZEKIEL	
20:33-38	135
ZECHARIAH	
12:10-14	131
MALACHI	
2:16	74
MATTHEW	
3:11	113
5:31-32	74
7:1	46, 52
8:14-15	88
11:19	91
13:55	88
16:1	28
16:18	20, 136
17:20	118
18:15-17	52
19:1-12	74
19:5	71
19:10	74
19:11-12	81
25:1-30	135
25:13	141

25:31-46	135
26:26-30	97, 104
28:11-15	130
28:16-20	130
28:19	25
MARK	
1:4-8	113
7:4, 8	114
10:1-12	74
11:22	121
13:32	141
14:22-26	97, 104
16:11, 13-14	130
16:14-20	110
LUKE	
3:16-17	113
5:32	57
7:34	91
12:40, 46	141
15:17	54
16:18	74
16:24	114
18:34	130
22:14-23	97, 104
23:34	34
JOHN	
1:1	121
1:14	38
1:29	55
3	139
3:3	29
5	134
5:28-29	135
7:5	131
10	115, 129
10:18	129
12:24	138
13:26	114

14:2-3	105	19:1	146
14:3	140, 141	20:7	106
14:16	64	20:17	20
14:16-17	114	20:28	65
15	115	21:8-9	101
15:16	20	22:1	20
		22:3	32
ACTS		23:26	22
1:4-5	113	24:10	152
1:8	57	25:10-11	59
2	113	26:10	88
2:4	114	28:30-31	152
2:5-11	114		
3:11	34	ROMANS	
3:17	34	1:1-2	129
7:22	32	1:13	94
9:15-16	90	1:16	7, 148
13:5	44	1:18-32	62
13:21	95	1:32	62
14:14	20	2:25-29	78
15:13-21	89	5	115
15:23	22	5:12-21	134
16:1	78	6	37
16:1-3	78	6:1-2	52
16:12	11	6:23	30
16:21	148	8:9	38
17	91, 133	8:15-23	133
17:18	31	8:23	114
17:28	32	11:13	144
17:32	133	11:25-27	131
18	89	12	37, 109
18:1-3	148	14	86, 115
18:1-18	10	14:8-12	41
18:8	20	15:25-27	144
18:9-10	10	16:1	13
18:12	12	16:23	7
18:14-17	59		
18:17	20	1 CORINTHIANS	
18:18	13	1:1-3	19
18:24	24, 146, 147	1:4-9	22
19	136, 145	1:7	23

1:9	23	4:14-21	49
1:10-17	23	4:15	19, 41, 87
1:11	16	5:1-8	51
1:12	146	5:3	46
1:17	25, 26	5:6	54
1:18-25	26	5:7	54
1:18	27	5:9-13	55
1:20	27	5:9	55
1:21	28	5:9	56
1:25	29	5:11	57
1:26-31	29	6:1-8	58
2:1-5	30	6:4	59
2:2	7, 15, 24, 32, 129	6:9-20	60
2:6-13	33	6:11	7, 62
2:8	34	6:12	63
2:10	35	6:15	64
2:14-15	139	6:17	64
2:14-16	36	6:18	64
2:14	36	6:19	43, 79
2:15	37	7:1-24	81
2:16	38	7:1-9	69
3	46	7:1	16, 70
3:1-4	38, 124	7:2	81
3:1	37, 39	7:3	71
3:4-6, 22	146	7:4	72
3:5-10	40	7:5	72
3:9	41	7:6	73
3:11-15	41	7:7	73, 88
3:13-15	41	7:8	73
3:14	41	7:10-16	73
3:15	41, 93	7:12	75
3:16-17	42	7:14	76
3:18-23	43	7:15	76
4:1-5	44	7:17-24	77
4:1	44	7:18	78
4:5	46, 91	7:19	78
4:6-13	47	7:21	78
4:6	146	7:23	79
4:7	30, 48	7:25-40	79
4:9	49	7:25	70, 81
4:10	48	7:26	80

7:36-40	81	11:1	50, 99
7:36	82	11:2-16	100
7:39	76, 82	11:2	103
7:39-40	76, 82	11:10	102
8	84, 87	11:14	102
8:1-13	83	11:15	102
8:1	70	11:16	102
8:2	85	11:17-22	102
8:4-6	85	11:17	103
8:4	85	11:20	97
8:7	85	11:22	103
8:12	86	11:23-26	103
9	84, 143	11:23	121
9:1-18	86	11:26	105
9:1	87, 104	11:27-34	106
9:5	73	11:29	107
9:6	88	11:30	107
9:10	89	11:32	107
9:18	90	12–14	23
9:19-23	90	12	37, 109
9:22	31, 78	12:1-11	108
9:24-27	42, 92	12:1	70, 94
10	84, 86, 95	12:1, 4	111
10:1-13	93	12:12-31	112
10:1-4	94	12:12	115
10:1	94	12:13	94, 104, 114
10:2	94	12:29-30	116
10:3	94	13	122
10:5	94	13:1-13	116
10:6, 11, 12	95	13:1-3	117
10:7	95	13:4-8	117
10:14-22	96	13:7	118
10:16	97	13:8-13	110
10:21	97	13:9-13	117
10:23–11:1	97	14	116, 122
10:24	98	14:1-5	121
10:27	98	14:1	118
10:28	98	14:6-19	122
10:31	99	14:10-11	123
10:32	20, 91, 99	14:16	124
11	127	14:18	124

14:20-25	124	16:19	148
14:26-40	125	16:22	148
14:26	126	16:23-24	148
14:27	127		
14:28	127	2 CORINTHIANS	
14:32	127	1:8	94
14:34-35	101	2:4	56
14:34	127	2:6-7	54
14:35	127	5:1-10	41
14:37	127	5:1-9	140
14:40	126	5:1	141
15	115	5:1-2	139
15:1-11	128	5:10	46
15:1-5	15	5:17	29
15:1	149	6:14-18	76
15:2	129	8–9	144
15:5	130	10:1-6	50
15:7	130	11:2	115
15:9	131	12:9-10	116, 131
15:12-19	131		
15:12	129	GALATIANS	
15:19	133	1:2	20
15:20-28	133	1:8-9	148
15:27-28	135	1:11-12	104, 131
15:29-34	135	1:14	32
15:29	136	1:19	89, 130
15:35-50	137	2:3-5	78
15:39	138	2:11	91
15:41	138	3:27	25
15:42	139	5:9	54
15:45	139	5:16-24	118
15:51-58	139	5:23	127
15:58	141	6:1	52
16:1-4	143		
16:1	70	EPHESIANS	
16:5-11	144	1:7	65
16:7	145	1:13-14	114
16:8	20, 137, 145, 152	2	115, 116
16:12	70, 146	2:8-10	30
16:13-24	147	2:19-22	42
16:15	147	2:20	110

3:10	20
4	109, 116
4:1-6	111
4:7-16	110
4:30	114
5:7	90
5:32	71

PHILIPPIANS

1:19-26	152
1:22-24	38
3:12-14	42, 142
3:20-21	141

COLOSSIANS

1:14	65
3:17	99
4:16	56

1 THESSALONIANS

1:1	20
1:8-10	141
4:3	21
4:13-18	140
4:13	94
4:17	134, 141
5:23	139

2 THESSALONIANS

1:1	20
3:17	148

1 TIMOTHY

1:2	22
2:11-15	101, 127
4:12	145
5:14	82
5:22	90
6:20	23

2 TIMOTHY

1:2	22
2:15	93
2:21	21
2:22	64
3:15-17	36
3:15	125
3:16	15
4:6-8	152
4:20	116

TITUS

1:4	22
2:11-14	149
3:4-7	114
3:5	62
3:13	146

PHILEMON

22	152

HEBREWS

1:1	35
2	110
2:1-4	33, 110
2:1-3	119, 126
2:3	111
4:12	139
5:13-15	39
9:10	114
10:10-14	21
10:14	21
11:4	84
11:29	94
12:29	43
13:4	71

JAMES

1:1	21
3:1	116

1 PETER		4:8	120
1:12	102	4:8, 16	121
1:18-20	65	4:16	120
1:21	121	4:19	121
1:22-25	114	5:16	107
1:23	9		
2	115	2 JOHN	
2:4-5	42	10-11	58
3:1-2	77		
		JUDE	
2 PETER		6	59
1:20-21	36	19	37
2:4	59		
3:3-4	46	REVELATION	
		1:4	20
1 JOHN		1:7	131
1:9	107	1:20	102
2:19	129	19:13	114
2:28	42	20	134
3:1-3	21	20:5, 12	135
3:4	121	21	115
4:2-3	38	21:2, 9	71